Opening the Door of Faith

A Study Guide for Catechists and the New Evangelization

Opening the Door of Faith

A Study Guide for Catechists and the New Evangelization

Jem Sullivan, Ph.D.

Foreword by Cardinal Donald Wuerl

Our Sunday Visitor Publishing Division
Our Sunday Visitor, Inc.
Huntington, Indiana 46750

Nihil Obstat:
Msgr. Michael Heintz, Ph.D.
Censor Librorum

Imprimatur:
✠ Kevin C. Rhoades
Bishop of Fort Wayne-South Bend
August 27, 2012

The *Nihil Obstat* and *Imprimatur* are declarations that a work is free from doctrinal or moral error. It is not implied that those who have granted the *Nihil Obstat* and *Imprimatur* agree with the contents, opinions, or statements expressed.

This book is dedicated to my son, Benedict.

"I am the door; if anyone enters by me, he will be saved,
and will go in and out and find pasture."

John 10:9

"Go out into the whole world
and preach the Gospel to every creature."

Mark 16:15

"Whatever good work you begin to do,
beg of God with most earnest prayer to perfect it."

Rule of Saint Benedict, Prologue

"Christianity has its starting point
in the Incarnation of the Word …
it is not simply a case of man seeking God,
but of God who comes in Person to speak
to man of himself,
and to show him the path by which he may be reached."

Blessed Pope John Paul II, Tertio Millenio Adveniente, 6

"The purpose of our lives is to reveal God to men.
And only where God is seen does life truly begin.
Only when we meet the living God in Christ
do we know what life is."

Pope Benedict XVI, Homily at the Mass
for the Inauguration of the Pontificate *(April 24, 2005)*

CONTENTS

FOREWORD

In his Apostolic Letter *Porta Fidei,* announcing a Year of Faith, Pope Benedict XVI calls the entire Church "to an authentic and renewed conversion to the Lord." All the faithful are invited to join in this graced time of reflection and rediscovery of the joy and beauty of faith in Jesus Christ. In this celebration of a Year of Faith, all baptized Catholics are also invited to actively become a part of the new evangelization, a central motif in the pontificate of Pope Benedict XVI.

At the heart of the new evangelization is the call to all of us believers to renew and deepen our faith, both intellectually and spiritually, with both heart and mind, in a way that renews our confidence in the truth of God's word spoken to us in his Church. Out of this should come a profound desire to share this Good News with others.

As you have read or heard about the new evangelization and prepared to celebrate the Year of Faith, you may have asked the question, "How do I respond to the Church's call to, 'give an account for the hope that is in you' (1 Peter 3:15)?" As a Catholic school teacher, you may wonder, "How does my instruction serve to open the door of faith to those I am privileged to teach?" As a catechist, you may ask, "How might the Church's call for a new evangelization serve as a 'moment of grace,' a fresh outpouring of the Holy Spirit, that renews my catechetical service to the parish community?"

In *Opening the Door of Faith: A Study Guide for Catechists and the New Evangelization,* Dr. Jem Sullivan invites the reader to reflect on answers to such questions. The book is offered primarily as a guide to catechists and teachers who stand on the front lines of the new evangelization. It is also aimed at assisting lay Catholics who, by virtue of Baptism, are meant to contribute actively to the new evangelization through their daily witness to the Gospel way of life.

This book affirms a Christ-centered foundation for all catechetical and faith formation activities. In the opening chapter, readers are invited to consider five ingredients of effective catechesis that serves the new evangelization. Catechists are given an opportunity to reflect on catechetical principles and best practices that can serve to open the "door of faith" to children, teenagers, young adults, and adults in faith formation programs.

When Pope Benedict XVI announced, in the context of Solemn Vespers for the Feasts of Saints Peter and Paul at the Basilica of Saint Paul Outside the Walls, his intention to form a new Vatican office to encourage and oversee the new evangelization, he described it as "re-proposing the Good News to those who have drifted away from the embrace of the faith." That evening, our Holy Father announced that he had decided to create a Pontifical Council whose principal task is to promote the new evangelization. The word that the Holy Father chose to describe the work identifies for us the very nature and task of the new evangelization. We are summoned, in the words of Pope Benedict, to "re-propose the perennial truth of Christ's Gospel."

The Pope further specified the work of the new evangelization as the proposal of Jesus Christ and his Gospel "in the countries where the first proclamation of the faith has already resonated and where churches with an ancient foundation exist that are experiencing the progressive secularization of society and a sort of 'eclipse of the sense of God.'"

In the chapter entitled "Proposing the Gospel Anew — Toward an *Evangelizing Catechesis*," the reader is challenged to consider what this activity means. The author reflects on elements of an "*evangelizing catechesis*" that draw on the essential and complementary relationship between evangelization and catechesis. She offers practical approaches to support a truly "*evangelizing catechesis*" along with questions for discussion and reflection.

In the next chapter, the author engages the question of how best to bridge faith and culture through the essential task of inculturating the Gospel in the lives of those who seek to know and live the Christian faith. Here, principles for an "*inculturated catechesis*" that serves the new evangelization are offered. The author also highlights catechetical responses to the influence of secularism, individualism, and relativism on those in faith formation programs and those on the periphery of the Church's life.

The final chapter of the book discusses the origin and purpose of the *Catechism of the Catholic Church* — as a means to celebrate the twentieth anniversary of its publication, which is drawing near. The *Catechism* remains an indispensable treasure and tool of effective catechesis in the new evangelization. To aid in the rediscovery of the *Catechism* as the authentic norm and treasure of faith, the author offers ten "best practices" to guide the use of the *Catechism*. This chapter may be used to outline a "study day" on the *Catechism*, which is encouraged in the *Note with Pastoral Recommendations for the Year of Faith*.

Finally, brief meditations on the Blessed Virgin Mary, under the title "Star of the New Evangelization," and the cover painting entitled *The Miraculous Draught of Fishes* are presented. The book concludes with a brief bibliography of Church documents and select resources on the new evangelization, for reference and further study.

Authentic catechesis precedes, accompanies, and enriches all new evangelization initiatives. The daily and weekly commitment of catechists and teachers of faith provides an indispensable support to the Church's evangelizing mission. Through systematic instruction in the content of the Catholic faith and joyful witness to its beauty and life-changing power, a renewal of catechesis in our time will be made possible. In preparing children for the Sacraments of First Eucharist and First Penance, and teenagers for the Sacrament of Confirmation; in instructing adult catechumens and those seeking full communion in the Church through the RCIA; and in evangelizing those who have fallen away from the practice of the faith, a catechist extends the love of God revealed in Jesus Christ to people of every generation, culture, and place.

Opening the Door of Faith: A Study Guide for Catechists and the New Evangelization will serve as a helpful companion and guide to anyone who strives to propose the Gospel anew through an evangelizing and inculturated catechesis. Readers of this book will be encouraged to a renewed love of catechetical service in support of the Church's evangelizing mission. Whether you are an experienced catechist with many years of catechetical leadership, a seasoned Catholic school religious education teacher, or a new volunteer catechist, you will find, in these pages, inspiration and encouragement for your service of the Church.

Opening the Door of Faith: A Study Guide for Catechists and the New Evangelization is a blessing for Catholics in general, and particularly for catechists who seek to understand and put into practice their vital role in the new evangelization. It is a great pleasure for me to recommend this book as a companion piece for all who try to pass on the Catholic faith. It is a welcome *vademecum* in the effort to rekindle the embers of faith that for some may have grown cold and to fan into flame those same embers that need encouragement. May your reading of this book bring about a fresh Spirit-filled joy and renewed enthusiasm for witnessing to the truth and beauty of the Catholic faith. For, in the words of Pope Benedict XVI:

> There is nothing more beautiful than to be surprised by the Gospel,
> by the encounter with Christ. There is nothing more beautiful than to
> know Him, and to speak to others of our friendship with Him. (Homily
> at the Mass for the Inauguration of the Pontificate, April 24, 2005)

HIS EMINENCE CARDINAL DONALD WUERL
ARCHBISHOP OF WASHINGTON

Forming Catechists and Teachers for the New Evangelization

The year 2012 will mark several milestones in the Catholic Church. During this year the Church celebrates the twentieth anniversary of the publication of the *Catechism of the Catholic Church*. The year also marks the fiftieth anniversary of the opening of the Second Vatican Council, held in Rome from 1962 to 1965. In October 2012, a Synod of Bishops gathers in Rome to consider possibilities and challenges for the transmission of the faith in the new evangelization. And following the establishment of a new Pontifical Council for the New Evangelization, Pope Benedict XVI invites the Church to celebrate a Year of Faith, to begin on October 11, 2012.

What significance do these events have for catechists, evangelists, teachers, and those responsible for faith formation? The book in your hands aims to answer that question.

As a pastor, a parent, a catechist or Catholic school religion teacher, you have no doubt heard or read about the "new evangelization," consistently called for by Pope Benedict XVI and by Blessed Pope John Paul II. Some questions you might ask:

- How do I become a catechist of the new evangelization?

- How does my educational and catechetical ministry open the door of faith to those I am privileged to catechize and form in the Church's faith?

- How do I respond to the Church's call to witness to faith at home, in the workplace, in my neighborhood and community?

- How might the Church's call for a new evangelization encourage a renewed catechesis aimed at re-proposing the Gospel to those who may have fallen away from the practice of the Catholic faith?

Our search for answers to such questions rests on the premise that the new evangelization is, in fact, a graced opportunity for a renewal of catechesis in our time.

This book begins by exploring the term, "new evangelization," from theological and catechetical perspectives. Then concrete, practical, and pastoral approaches are offered to assist and support catechists and teachers in their vital role as catalysts of the new evangelization.

Who would benefit from these pages? Each and every Catholic is invited to take up anew their baptismal call to participate in the new evangelization. So the reflections in this book are offered to Catholic lay men and women who are all evangelizers, by reason of their Baptism, Confirmation, and Eucharist. It invites a Catholic lay person to reflect on and understand how they are to know, to live, and to witness to their faith in Jesus Christ, who stands at the heart of the new evangelization. The particular audience that this book aims to reach is pastors, catechists, evangelists, teachers, directors and coordinators of religious education and evangelization programs, RCIA leaders and catechists, and those engaged in evangelization outreach programs to inactive Catholics. To them this book is offered as one roadmap to guide their dedicated and daily efforts on the front lines of the new evangelization. While catechist formation is the specific context in mind, all are invited to renew their baptismal commitment to be active instruments of the new evangelization.

In Chapter One, the reader is invited to consider the "new evangelization" through a sustained reflection on one image offered by Pope Benedict XVI in a homily given during his Apostolic Visit to the United States in 2008. Drawn from this image, five elements of catechesis in the new evangelization are identified and discussed. Catechists are given an opportunity to reflect on catechetical principles and practices that open the "door of faith" to those they serve in catechetical programs and in the classroom. In Chapter Two, catechists are encouraged to consider the challenge of presenting an *"evangelizing catechesis,"* that respects the essential relationship between evangelization and catechesis. Practical approaches to support a truly *"evangelizing catechesis"* are offered, along with questions for discussion and reflection. Then in Chapter Three, theological principles and practical approaches for an *"inculturated catechesis"* that serves the new evangelization are offered. Finally, in Chapter Four, themes to guide a "study day" on the *Catechism of the Catholic Church,* the essential catechetical tool in the new evangelization, are discussed. Then brief meditations on Mary, Star of the New Evangelization, and the book cover art by Jacopo Bassano entitled *The Miraculous Draught of Fishes* are presented. The book concludes with a select bibliography of Church documents and resources on the new evangelization, for reference and further study.

An Invitation

This book is written by a catechist and a teacher for catechists and teachers of faith. A basic assumption of the author is that the call to each catechist to share in and extend the Church's catechetical mission is a profound gift. This sharing in the Church's catechetical efforts is also a responsibility and task, entrusted to every catechist. The book also assumes that the distinct role of catechists in the new evangelization supports, deepens, and extends the active role that every baptized Catholic takes in the Church's evangelizing mission.

The chapters of this book may be used as modules for a series of catechist formation sessions for large or small groups or catechetical study and reflection days. The catechetical principles and pastoral approaches offered in these pages may also serve in the formation of individual volunteer catechists, catechetical leaders, and Catholic school religious education teachers. Reflections on the Church's evangelizing and catechetical mission make an ideal companion for ongoing catechist certification or catechist enrichment. In particular, the themes covered in chapter four may be used as a practical guide to planning a catechetical study day on the *Catechism of the Catholic Church.*

Each chapter presents theological, catechetical, and pastoral principles and includes discussion questions, space for personal reflection, and additional resources for further reading. It is humbly offered to pastors, parents, catechists, and teachers engaged in the faith formation of children, teenagers, young adults, and adults, whether they are active Catholics, nominal or "cultural" Catholics, those who, for one reason or another, no longer participate actively in the Church's life, or those who desire to join the family of the Catholic Church.

CHAPTER ONE

THE NEW EVANGELIZATION OPENING THE "DOOR OF FAITH"

What is the "new evangelization"? How will the "new evangelization" find concrete expression and pastoral application in America? Is the "new evangelization" reserved only for those we call "evangelists"? What is the relationship of catechesis to evangelization, old and new? And how do catechists, who are on the front lines of the "new evangelization," prepare to take their part as effective agents of the Church's evangelizing mission?

These are some of the questions that this book will consider. In this chapter, we will begin by reflecting on the phrase, "new evangelization," within the broader context of the Church's permanent evangelizing mission. We begin by affirming that there are three moments in evangelization, namely the Church's permanent evangelization, the evangelization *ad gentes,* which is the initial proclamation of the Gospel in missionary activity, and the "new evangelization" that addresses particularly those baptized Christians who have drifted from the practice of the Catholic faith and the communion of the Church.

Then we will consider one image that serves to illustrate and highlight various catechetical challenges in the "new evangelization." Marks of effective catechesis that serves the new evangelization based on this image are then proposed. To guide your reflections further you will find space for reflection as well as discussion questions at the end of the chapter.

The new evangelization and the Church's "permanent evangelization"

Evangelization is as old as the Church. In fact, in every age, even to the present day, each baptized Catholic shares in the fruits of the Church's evangelizing mission. As a catechist, your own faith journey most likely began and continues to be nourished in the evangelizing heart of the Church. For, as then Cardinal Joseph Ratzinger noted in an address to catechists and religious educators given during the Jubilee Year 2000:

"The Church always evangelizes and has never interrupted the path of evangelization. She celebrates the Eucharistic mystery every day, administers the Sacraments, proclaims the word of life — the Word of God, and commits herself to the causes of justice and charity ... this evangelization bears fruit. It gives light and joy, it gives the path of life to many people, many others live, often unknowingly, off the light and the warmth that radiate from this permanent evangelization." [1]

The uninterrupted and "permanent evangelization" of the Church is the abiding context for taking up the call for a "new evangelization." So, as catechists and teachers of faith, we begin these reflections with a sense of gratitude. A catechist is grateful that his or her call to serve the Church's catechetical and educational mission is sustained continually by the Church's permanent evangelizing mission. This "permanent evangelization" includes the Church's proclamation of God's Word, the profession of faith in the Creed, the celebration of the Sacraments, and action that serves charity and justice rooted in the Commandments and the Beatitudes.

So we begin by situating the "new evangelization" within the Church's perennial evangelizing mission. Why? Because without the Church's two thousand year old evangelizing presence in every age and place, the "new evangelization" may be reduced easily to yet another Church program, whose novelty will fade eventually over time. More importantly, "the new evangelization is not a matter of redoing something that has been inadequately done or has not achieved its purpose, as if the new activity were an implicit judgment on the failure of the first evangelization." [2] It is only within the Church's ongoing and "permanent evangelization" that we properly understand the call of the "new evangelization."

One of the highpoints in the Church's perennial evangelization is the "golden age" of the early Church, also known as the patristic age or the age of the Fathers of the Church. Evangelization played no small part in the wildfire spread of Christianity in the first four centuries of the Church's life. As we look to catechesis in the new evangelization, we can learn much from that "golden age" in catechesis and evangelization, as summarized by Rodney Stark in this way:

Because Christianity was a mass movement, rooted in a highly committed rank and file, it had the advantage of the best of all marketing techniques: person-to-person influence. Christianity did not grow because of miracle working in the marketplaces (although there may have been much of that going on), or because Constantine said it should, or even because the martyrs gave it such credibility. It grew because Christians constituted an intense community, able to generate the "invincible obstinacy" that so offended the younger Pliny but yielded immense religious rewards. And the primary means of its growth was through the united and motivated efforts of the growing number of Christian believers, who invited their friends, relatives, and neighbors to share the "good news." [3]

Vatican II — an original moment in the "new evangelization"

The seeds of the "new evangelization" may be traced back some fifty years ago to the event of the Second Vatican Council (1962–1965). In fact, it could be said that the Second Vatican Council was itself the original moment in the new evangelization. As the Council began, Blessed Pope John XXIII prayed earnestly for a "new Pentecost" that would "vivify the temporal order with the light of Christ," and "bring the modern world into contact with the vivifying and perennial energies of the Gospel."[4] In his Opening Speech to the Council, the Pope highlighted the need for the Church to consider new ways to propose the Gospel message to the world of today, while he affirmed that, "the substance of the ancient doctrine of the deposit of faith is one thing, and the way in which it is presented is another." This *aggiornamento*, or updating, called for by Pope John XXIII, urged a renewed evangelization by which the Church "opens the fountain of her life-giving doctrine which allows men, enlightened by the light of Christ, to understand well what they really are, what their lofty dignity and their purpose are, and finally, through her children, she spreads everywhere the fullness of Christian charity."[5] It can be argued that the original impetus and the entire program of Vatican II was aimed at a revitalization of the Church's evangelizing mission, in response to a rapidly changing world.

Through its sixteen documents the Second Vatican Council sounded the first note in a fresh symphony of theological reflection and pastoral initiatives to bring the Gospel of Jesus Christ to the world of today. Within a "hermeneutic of continuity" with the twenty Church councils that came before it, this Council's vision for a new evangelization drew nourishment from the deep roots of the Church's two-thousand-year-old "deposit of faith." This "deposit of faith," or Sacred Tradition, is summarized in the *Catechism of the Catholic Church*.

The call for a new evangelization traces back to the command of Jesus to his apostles: "Go therefore and make disciples of all nations, baptizing them in the name of the Father and of the Son and of the Holy Spirit, teaching them to observe all that I commanded you." (Matthew 29:19–20). It is this charge of Jesus to his apostles that continues, across the centuries, even in our time in the new evangelization. In every age of the Church bishops, as successors of the apostles, together with priests, consecrated religious, and laity, respond to Jesus' command, in and through the Church's evangelizing presence and mission.

The renewed emphasis on evangelization, begun at Vatican II, would be echoed subsequently and consistently by Pope Paul VI, Blessed Pope John Paul II, and Pope Benedict XVI. In a foundational document, the Apostolic Exhortation "On Evangelization in the Modern World" (*Evangelii Nuntiandi*), Pope Paul VI summarized the goal of evangelization in this way:

> For the Church, evangelizing means bringing the Good News into all the strata of humanity, and through its influence transforming human-

ity from within and making it new.... To evangelize is first of all to bear witness, in a simple and direct way, to God revealed by Jesus Christ, in the Holy Spirit, to bear witness that in His Son, God has loved the world — that in His Incarnate Word He has given being to all things and has called men to eternal life.... Evangelization will always contain — as the foundation, center, and at the same time, the summit of its dynamism — a clear proclamation that, in Jesus Christ, the Son of God made man, who died and rose from the dead, salvation is offered to all men, as a gift of God's grace and mercy. [6]

The new evangelization — "new ardor, method, and expression"

It was Blessed Pope John Paul II who first spoke of a "new evangelization," some thirty years ago. The Holy Father noted that "the call for a great re-launching of evangelization enters into the present life of the Church in a number of ways. In truth, it has never been absent." [7] Blessed Pope John Paul II's initial and subsequent calls now find concrete expression in various initiatives of Pope Benedict XVI, who has made the new evangelization one of the defining themes of his papacy. While on a 1979 visit to his native land, Poland, Blessed Pope John Paul II spoke, with deep hope, of "a new evangelization (that) has begun." Four years later, in his Opening Address to the Sixth General Assembly of CELAM in Haiti (the Latin American Episcopal Council), Blessed Pope John Paul II highlighted the need for a "new evangelization, new in its ardor, method, and expression." [8]

> This sacred Council ... wishes to unite the efforts of all the faithful, so that the people of God, following the narrow way of the Cross, might everywhere spread the kingdom of Christ ... and prepare the way for His coming.
>
> Vatican II, Decree on the Church's Missionary Activity, *Ad Gentes*, 1

In creating the Pontifical Council for the Promotion of the New Evangelization in June 2010, Pope Benedict XVI noted that its principal task would be to promote "a renewed evangelization in the countries where the first proclamation of faith has already resonated and where Churches with an ancient foundation exist but are experiencing the progressive secularization of society ... which poses a challenge to finding appropriate ways to propose anew the perennial truths of Christ's Gospel." [9] The "new evangelization" does not imply a "new Gospel," since "Jesus Christ is the same yesterday, today and forever" (Hebrews 13:8). Rather, the new evangelization is "a new response to the needs of humanity and people today in a manner adapted to the signs of the times and to the new situations in cultures, which are the basis of our personal identity and the places where we seek the meaning of our existence." [10]

Understanding the new evangelization through an image

Following the Second Vatican Council, Catholics have been invited to rediscover their identity and mission as evangelists. In the past fifty years one may find numerous Church documents, papal exhortations, and addresses on the new evangelization. These are rich resources for catechists seeking to learn more about the relationship of catechesis to the new evangelization. A select bibliography of such resources is included at the end of this book for your reference and further reading. However, even in these numerous Church resources from the past fifty years no single definition of the new evangelization emerges. Why is that?

> To evangelize is first of all to bear witness, in a simple and direct way, to God revealed by Jesus Christ, in the Holy Spirit, to bear witness that in His Son, God has loved the world — that in His Incarnate Word He has given being to all things and has called men to eternal life.
>
> Pope Paul VI, *Evangelii Nuntiandi*

The new evangelization is a many-faceted reality with multiple moments, aspects and ingredients. And no one definition of the new evangelization exists precisely because the Church's evangelizing mission cannot be reduced to a single description, a concise formula, or a specific diocesan or parish program. The new evangelization encompasses the entire life and mission of the Church and the whole life of faith in Jesus Christ. Its content is the whole of the Gospel proposed as the living communication of the mystery of God. It cannot be limited to one initiative, program, or outreach. Rather it permeates everything that the Church is and does. It shapes and informs the whole reality of the Church in the world. Like a drop of ink that colors the entire cup of water, the new evangelization saturates every aspect of the Church's faith and life.

As Cardinal Donald Wuerl notes in his Pastoral Letter on the New Evangelization, *Disciples of the Lord: Sharing the Vision,* "the new evangelization is much more an outlook on life than it is a program. While there will be programmatic aspects to this effort to bring new zest to what has gone stale and new energy to what has gone flat, so much of what we are embarking on in this process is, essentially, that turning and returning to the Lord that is at the heart of Christian conversion.... For this reason, the new evangelization is not a passing project, short-lived slogan or fleeting theme. It is not a transitory program, but a permanent mystery." [1]

> The term evangelization has a very rich meaning. In the broad sense, it sums up the Church's entire mission: her whole life consists in accomplishing the *traditio Evangelii*, the proclamation and handing on of the Gospel, which is "the power of God for the salvation of everyone who believes" (Romans 1:16) and which, in the final essence, is identified with Jesus Christ himself (cf. 1 Cor 1:24). Understood in this way, evangelization is aimed at all of humanity. In any case, to *evangelize* does not mean to teach a doctrine, but to proclaim Jesus Christ by one's words and actions, that is, to make oneself an instrument of his presence and action in the world.
>
> Congregation for the Doctrine of the Faith, *Doctrinal Note on Some Aspects of Evangelization, December 2007*

It stands to reason then that this multi-faceted reality is perhaps better understood through an image, rather than a single verbal or written definition. As a catechist or teacher you know well that one good image is often capable of explaining and evoking deep and multiple meanings, contained or hinted at within a single definition. For this reason reflecting on an image for the "new evangelization" is one effective way to understand its rich reality and mystery.

Our consideration of some definitions of the "new evangelization," presented later in this chapter, will be contextualized within this reflection on an image that evokes its meaning. Like any illustration this one image is limited. It does, however, paint a vivid and memorable picture of the tasks, the goals, and the challenges of the "new evangelization."

"Seeing with the eyes of faith"

During his 2008 Apostolic Visit to the United States, Pope Benedict XVI celebrated Mass in Saint Patrick's Cathedral in New York City. In his homily, the Pope drew attention to the splendor of that cathedral to evoke the beauty and unity of the Catholic faith itself. A cathedral, such as Saint Patrick's, with its sacred architecture and art, reflects in stone and stained glass the rich variety of gifts within the one Body of Christ.

Imagine for a moment that you are standing in front of a beautiful cathedral. Perhaps it is the diocesan cathedral in your home city, or a cathedral you once visited on pilgrimage, in this country or abroad. Perhaps the cathedral was built as a soaring Gothic church, a sturdy Romanesque edifice, or a Byzantine basilica. Whatever its architectural style, the sheer beauty and immensity of the cathedral is awe-inspiring. Yet your experience of the cathedral from the outside is limited to the immense exterior stone or concrete walls, the grey stained glass windows, and the decorated façade. From the outside, the cathedral can appear distant, imposing, even overbearing.

Photo by Michael Hoyt

Photo by
Jem Sullivan

At the same time its beauty intrigues, it compels, it invites. And it is only by entering through its doors and by stepping into the sacred interior space that one can experience its inner beauty and harmony.

It is this image of entering into a beautiful cathedral that Pope Benedict XVI explored in his homily at Saint Patrick's Cathedral in 2008. The Holy Father's reflection offers to catechists a poignant image for the "new evangelization" in these words:

> The first has to do with the stained glass windows, which flood the interior with mystic light. From the outside, those windows are dark, heavy, even dreary. But once one enters the Church, they suddenly come alive; reflecting the light passing through them, they reveal all their splendor. Many writers — here in America we can think of Nathaniel Hawthorne — have used the image of stained glass to illustrate the mystery of the Church herself. It is only from the inside, from the experience of faith and ecclesial life, that we see the Church as she truly is: flooded with grace, resplendent in beauty, adorned by the manifold gifts of the Spirit. It follows that we, who live the life of grace within the Church's communion, are called to draw all people into this mystery of light. [12]

Photo by Rev. Terry
Ehrman, C.S.C.

To "draw all people into this mystery of light," in the words of Pope Benedict XVI, captures, in a nutshell, the essence of the "new evangelization" as the mission of every baptized Christian. And, based on this image, one may outline certain characteristics and features of catechetical ministry that support the "new evangelization." As you consider these elements you are invited to add your own insight based on your reflection on this image.

Catechetical dimensions of the new evangelization

The new evangelization includes, but is not limited to, the following features or elements, drawn from the image of passing through the doors of a beautiful cathedral. These elements of the new evangelization may also be viewed as a series of catechetical "checkpoints" for a catechist to consider while preparing for a catechetical session or presentation. Here are some catechetical dimensions of the new evangelization drawn from the image of entering a beautiful cathedral:

1. Catechesis in the new evangelization invites others to encounter God as a "mystery of light." But how are we to understand this "mystery of light" to which we are to draw all people?

The "mystery of light" to which a catechist draws others is nothing less than divine grace in which the life of every Christian begins and ends. Catechesis that serves the new evangelization takes, as its starting point, the reality of God, and the divine initiative of love, experienced as grace. When a catechist proposes, teaches, and witnesses to the reality of God he or she does not present an abstract system of beliefs and propositions. To proclaim God is to introduce others into a relationship with God. "Faith grows when it is lived as an experience of love received and when it is communicated as an experience of grace and joy. It makes us fruitful, because it expands our hearts in hope and enables us to bear life-giving witness." [13]

To witness to the reality of God is to invite others into a relationship with Him, who is experienced as the source of divine light and new life. God desires friendship and communion with the crown of his creation, that is, human persons made in the divine image and likeness. This desire of God that all of creation share in the love and unity of the divine community of the Father, the Son, and the Holy Spirit, is the reason why His grace is active in human history and in human hearts. Flowing from this "divine pedagogy," a catechist presents faith as an experience of divine love received as unmerited grace and leading to lasting and deep joy.

Blessed Pope John Paul II reminded us of "the duty of praise." This is the point of departure for every genuine response of faith to the revelation of God in Christ. "Christianity is grace; it is the wonder of a God who is not satisfied with creating the world and man, but puts himself on the same level as the creature he has made … (and) 'in these last days … he has spoken to us by a Son' (Hebrews 1:1–2)." (Blessed Pope John Paul II, *Novo Millenio Ineunte*, 4)

The image of light streaming into a cathedral then is a powerful metaphor for the reality of God's love in the world. For just as rays of light that filter through the stained glass windows of a cathedral come from outside, from beyond the church building itself, the reality of God's existence and divine grace breaks into human experience, as a sheer gift of God's love and mercy. Human ingenuity or creativity, however advanced, can never create the gift of God's grace. Without light streaming from the outside through the stained glass windows into the cathedral interior the interior space is enveloped in shadows, just as alienation, confusion, and darkness follow wherever the light of God's grace is obscured or extinguished.

Grace is free, it is unmerited, it is not created by human hands or minds. God's grace originates in the reality of God, and it is transcendent. And like light itself, grace is a mystery.

Let us reflect a bit further on this mystery of grace, that is the starting point of catechesis in the new evangelization. Grace is the outpouring of divine love and life; the saving action of God that flows into the life of every person who is catechized and formed in the faith of the Church. The reality of grace flows from God's desire for our friendship and our salvation. And this communion with God, that is the gift of grace, is made possible through His only Son, Jesus Christ, in the power of the Holy Spirit. Ultimately, grace is God's free and loving invitation to every human person to partake of the Trinitarian mystery of divine love. The Church, the Body of Christ, is the visible means through which this divine grace permeates the world.

> With you is the fountain of life,
> and in your light we see light.
>
> Psalm 36:10

In Baptism, the gift of this divine life is given to all so that those illumined by faith may live as "children of God, and if children, then heirs, heirs of God and joint heirs with Christ. (Romans 8:17). As grace draws each person into the community of the divine persons of the Trinity, the Father, the Son, and the Holy Spirit, in the community of the Church, faith becomes the response of the whole human person to this invitation of grace.

This communion, or friendship with God, begins at Baptism as a gift of faith. Through faith, the whole range of a person's relationships is graced by the order and the light of God's own life and love. In this way, the experience of alienation as confusion, darkness, or despair is transformed into an encounter with God's love and presence, His kingdom on earth.

> Grace is a participation in the life of God. It introduces us into the intimacy of Trinitarian life ... this vocation to eternal life is supernatural. It depends entirely on God's gratuitous initiative, for he alone can reveal and give himself ... grace precedes, prepares, and elicits the free response of man. Grace responds to the deepest yearnings of human freedom, calls freedom to cooperate with it, and perfects freedom.
>
> CCC 1997, 1998, 2022

Catechesis in the new evangelization therefore returns to the foundational reality of the grace of God as "the most present and decisive reality in each and every act of my life, in each and every moment of history." This initial "catechetical moment" is made necessary by the fact that so many people, even Christians and those in our catechetical formation programs, "often live as if God did not exist. We live according to the slogan: God does not exist, and if he exists, he does not belong."[14] For this reason the new evangelization requires that a catechist clearly and lovingly proclaim the reality and revelation of God, experienced as a transformative grace, or "mystery of light," shining into the world. In this way, catechesis serves "the new evangelization (that) is primarily a spiritual activity capable of recapturing in our times the courage and forcefulness of the first Christians and first missionaries."[15]

A catechist may ask the question, "How does my catechetical ministry lead others to deeper faith and love experienced as an encounter with the 'mystery of light,' that is God's grace?"

_____

_____

_____

_____

2. Catechesis in the new evangelization centers on Christ, the light of the world.
We encounter the fullness of God's grace, understood as the "mystery of light" that shines into the world, in the Person of Jesus Christ. The Second Vatican Council reminded us: "Christ is the Light of nations," and the Church "eagerly desires, by proclaiming the Gospel to every creature (Mark 16:15) to bring the light of Christ to all people." [16] It is Jesus Christ who radiates into the world and into our lives the light of God's love. And it is only in the light of the life and person of Christ that we see, with the "eyes of faith," our true dignity as sons and daughters of God, made in the divine image and likeness. In the light of Christ's life and saving mission, each human person is invited to discover the meaning, dignity, and purpose of their life in relationship to God. In the words of Blessed Pope John Paul II: "Jesus Christ is the answer to the question that is every human person."

> This clarification was necessary in order to avoid any danger of a Pelagian interpretation. This danger already existed in the time of Saint Augustine, and seems to be surfacing again in our time. Pelagius asserted that even without divine grace, man could lead a good and happy life. Divine grace, therefore, was not necessary for him. But the truth is that man is actually called to salvation; that a good life is the condition of salvation; and that salvation cannot be attained without the help of grace.
>
> Blessed Pope John Paul II,
> _Crossing the Threshold of Hope_

Catechesis that serves the new evangelization invites others into an experience of faith in Jesus Christ, who stands at the center of catechetical ministry. A catechist never tires of returning, time and time again, to the life and saving mission of Jesus Christ, as the center of his or her catechetical ministry. This _Christocentric_ foundation of all catechesis was affirmed by Blessed Pope John Paul II in his Apostolic Exhortation _Catechesi Tradendae_, 5, in this way:

> At the heart of catechesis we find, in essence, a Person, the Person of Jesus of Nazareth, "the only Son from the Father … full of grace and truth,"(9) who suffered and died for us and who now, after rising, is living with us forever. It is Jesus who is "the way, and the truth, and the life,"(10) and Christian living consists in following Christ, the _sequela Christi_.… The primary and essential object of catechesis is, to use

an expression dear to St. Paul and also to contemporary theology, "the mystery of Christ." Catechizing is in a way to lead a person to study this mystery in all its dimensions ... accordingly, the definitive aim of catechesis is to put people not only in touch but in communion, in intimacy, with Jesus Christ: only He can lead us to the love of the Father in the Spirit and make us share in the life of the Holy Trinity.

Every religious tradition involves the human search for God. Christianity rests on this fundamental affirmation: that God, out of divine love, comes in search of humanity. Revelation is God's self-communication that reaches its fullness in the sending of His Son, the Word made flesh, Jesus Christ, who is the incarnate and personal face of God's love. For, "Christianity has its starting point in the Incarnation of the Word ... it is not simply a case of man seeking God, but of God who comes in Person to speak to man of himself, and to show him the path by which he may be reached." [17]

The centrality of Jesus Christ in the catechetical task can never be emphasized enough. From time to time, catechists do well to ask: "Do I really believe that Jesus is the Son of God?" "Is His divine person, his life, death, and resurrection the fundamental conviction of my life and ministry?" "Do I experience the joy of believing in Jesus Christ?" The effectiveness and "success" of catechetical ministry in the new evangelization depends on the answers that a catechist gives to these questions.

As Cardinal Donald Wuerl notes in his Pastoral Letter on the New Evangelization, *Disciples of the Lord: Sharing the Vision,* "the first movement of any evangelization originates not in a program, but in a Person, Jesus Christ, the Son of God. The Church maintains that '(I)t is the same Lord Jesus Christ who, present, in his Church, goes before the work of evangelizers, accompanies it, follows it, and makes their labor bear fruit; what took place at the origins of Christian history continues through its entire course.'" [18]

Christ Jesus is the inspiration, the goal, and the measure of "success" of every catechetical moment and faith formation program. For "in catechesis it is Christ, the Incarnate Word and Son of God, who is taught — everything else is taught with reference to Him — and it is Christ alone who teaches — anyone else teaches to the extent that he is Christ's spokesman, enabling Christ to teach with his lips." [19]

Catechists of the new evangelization employ various catechetical methodologies, inspired by the "pedagogy of God," with the aim of drawing others to know, love, and serve Jesus Christ, experienced as *the* light that comes from God. Just as light illumines everything it touches in the interior of a cathedral, so too does the light of Christ illumine the world, the Church, and every human heart and mind. Through catechetical formation, a catechist opens the "door of faith" so that others may experience God's grace revealed in Jesus Christ, as a light that shines into the world, in and through the Church, into their daily lives.

Faith in Jesus Christ is received as a light for the path of life, as divine grace. As the Psalmist affirms, "Your word, O Lord, is a lamp to my feet, and a light to my path."

(Ps 119:105). And from the catechist's own lived faith, experienced as a light that illumines the whole of one's life, radiates the various forms and levels of catechetical formation, instruction, and witness to the person of Jesus Christ. In this way, catechetical formation is fundamentally an invitation to encounter the life and teachings of Jesus, the Incarnate Word of God.

For a catechist the image of Christ the Teacher is at once, "majestic and familiar, impressive and reassuring." As catechists prepare for each catechetical session they do well to consider how they imitate and extend the image of Christ the Teacher to those they form in faith. A catechist draws inspiration and wisdom from:

> the whole of Christ's life (that) was a continual teaching: His silences, His miracles, His gestures, His prayer, His love for people, His special affection for the little and the poor, His acceptance of the total sacrifice on the cross for the redemption of the world, and His resurrection … Christ, the Teacher who reveals God to man and man to himself, the Teacher who saves, sanctifies and guides, who lives, who speaks, rouses, moves, redresses, judges, forgives, and goes with us day by day on the path of history … only in deep communion with Him will catechists find light and strength for an authentic, desirable renewal of catechesis.[20]

> "You are the light of the world … your light must shine before all." (Matthew 5:14, 16)…. Ask yourselves: Do I believe these words of Jesus in the Gospel? Jesus is calling you *the light of the world.* He is asking you to let your light shine before others … *but only if you are with Jesus can you share his light and be a light to the world* … because Jesus is the Light, we too become light when we proclaim him. This is the heart of the Christian mission to which each of you has been called through Baptism and Confirmation. *You are called to make the light of Christ shine brightly in the world.*
>
> Blessed Pope John Paul II, Homily to Youth, January 26, 1999

In preparing for a catechetical session, a catechist may pose this question: "How does each catechetical session I prepare for and each catechetical theme that I present serve as an invitation to experience the transforming power of divine grace, radiating from the life, death and resurrection of Jesus Christ?"

_____

_____

_____

_____

> The Church brings Christ, *the key to understanding that great and fundamental reality that is man.* For man cannot be fully understood without Christ. Or rather, man is incapable of understanding himself fully without Christ. He cannot understand who he is, nor what his true dignity is, nor what his vocation is, nor what his final end is. He cannot understand any of this without Christ.
>
> Blessed Pope John Paul II, Homily at Victory Square, Warsaw, June 2, 1979

Above all, the witness of holiness is necessary, if the light of truth is to reach all human beings. If the word is contradicted by behavior, its acceptance will be difficult. However, even witness by itself is not enough "because even the finest witness will prove ineffective in the long run, if it is not explained, justified — what Peter called 'giving a reason for the hope that is in you' (1 Peter 3:15) — and made explicit by a clear and unequivocal proclamation of the Lord Jesus."

Doctrinal Note on Some Aspects of Evangelization, 11

3. Catechesis in the new evangelization is rooted in a catechist's "full, conscious, and active participation"[21] in the Church's life and in ongoing conversion.

Catechesis in the new evangelization draws others into the life of the Christian community through the catechist's example of full, conscious, and active participation in the Church's life. The whole life of a catechist is to be illumined by the light of faith. Conversion is the daily and lifelong journey by which this illumination of life takes place. Ongoing conversion of both the catechist and the one being catechized is, first and foremost, a work of "the Holy Spirit, the principal agent of evangelization."[22] From full, conscious, and active participation in the Church's life a catechist grows in understanding of the truths of faith and their lived expression. Through daily conversion of life the joy and peace that comes from faith is deepened and grows.

In this way, a catechist's interior experience of faith leads to deep conviction and to love for the faith of the Church. From the catechist's convictions and full participation in the Church's life, the light of Christ radiates into the lives of those he or she is privileged to form in faith. For, "the evangelizing mission of the Church passes through charity, nourished by prayer and listening to God's word." [23]

The Greek word for converting means: to rethink — to question one's own and common way of living; to allow God to enter into the criteria of one's life; to not merely judge according to current opinions. Thereby, to convert means: not to live as all the others live, not to do what all do, not feel justified in dubious, ambiguous, evil actions just because others do the same; begin to see one's life through the eyes of God…; not aiming at the judgment of the majority of men but on the justice of God — in other words, to look for a new style of life, a new life.

Cardinal Joseph Ratzinger, Address on the New Evangelization, 2000

As a catechist grows in the lived experience of faith they find wisdom and strength in its inner beauty, its organic unity, and its graced power to transform lives. Such daily conversion of heart and mind is an indispensable element of ongoing effectiveness as a catechist of the new evangelization. For "we ourselves cannot gather men. We must acquire them by God for God. All methods are empty without the foundation of prayer. The word of the announcement must always be drenched in an intense life of prayer…. Jesus did not redeem the world with beautiful words but with his suffering and death. His Passion is the inexhaustible source of life for the world, the Passion gives power to his words." [24]

In reflecting on this ecclesial dimension of catechesis in the new evangelization, we are also reminded that:

the transmission of the faith is never an individual, isolated undertaking, but a communal, ecclesial event. It must not consider responses as a matter of researching an effective plan of communication … instead these responses must be done as something which concerns the one called to perform this spiritual work. It must become what the Church is by her nature … by placing at the center of discussion the entire Church in all she is and all she does. Perhaps in this way, the problem of unfruitfulness in evangelization and catechesis today can be seen as an ecclesiological problem which concerns the Church's capacity, more or less, of becoming a real community, a true fraternity and a living body, and not a mechanical thing or enterprise.[25]

Conversion of life for a catechist is nourished by perseverance in the interior life of prayer and through daily reflection on God's Word and active participation in the Sacraments. From this interior experience of faith, as a personal and living reality, a catechist proposes the full content of faith. In the same way, the entire Christian community is being continually evangelized while it strives to be an evangelizing presence in the world.

The path of personal conversion pursued within the faith of the Church prepares a catechist to offer a joyful and genuine personal witness in each catechetical moment. Numerous opportunities to share one's personal witness to faith are presented to catechists in formal or informal catechetical moments. In the power of the Holy Spirit, "the principal agent of evangelization,"[26] a catechist becomes aware of and responds to these graced opportunities to offer personal testimony. The importance of a catechist's personal witness to the lived experience of the Church's life is thus highlighted:

> Evangelization is not only accomplished through public preaching of the Gospel nor solely through works of public relevance, but also by means of personal witness which is always very effective in spreading the Gospel. Indeed, "side by side with the collective proclamation of the Gospel, the other form of handing it on, from person to person, remains valid and important … it must not happen that the pressing need to proclaim the Good News to the multitudes should cause us to forget this form of proclamation whereby an individual's personal conscience is reached and touched by an entirely unique word that he receives from someone else … in transmitting the Gospel, word and witness of life go together.[27]

The need to pursue the path of ongoing personal conversion, nourished by the Church's faith and life, is well known to catechists and teachers of faith. Yet it merits reflection as we consider the elements of catechesis that serve the new evangelization. A catechist may pose the following questions: "How often do I give personal witness to faith in my catechetical ministry?" "How can my personal witness be further deepened through reflection on God's Word and participation in the Church's sacramental life?"

_____

_____

_____

_____

A Year of Faith is intended to contribute to a renewed conversion to the Lord Jesus and to the rediscovery of faith, so that the members of the Church will be credible and joy-filled witnesses to the Risen Lord in the world of today — capable of leading those many people who are seeking it to the "door of faith." This "door" opens wide man's gaze to Jesus Christ, present among us "always, until the end of the age" (Matthew 28:20).

Note with Pastoral Recommendations for the Year of Faith, Congregation for the Doctrine of the Faith, January 6, 2012

4. Catechesis in the new evangelization presents the "art of living in the Church." [28]

Many people today, even those in programs of catechetical formation and sacramental preparation, often experience the Catholic faith from the periphery, from an "outsider," or "near outsider" perspective. They are, as it were, standing outside the cathedral and may be observing, even admiring the beauty of the cathedral, but not experiencing it from within. Many in our catechetical programs may have been born, raised, and educated in a Catholic home and community. Yet they remain distant or lukewarm in their participation in the Church's life. They stand on the margins of the Gospel way of life. And they may even be only one or two steps from falling away entirely from the practice of the Catholic faith. One may consider himself "Catholic," but his way of thought, actions, and life are shaped and sustained by the surrounding culture, not the faith and life of the Church.

One of the prevailing secular assumptions about Christian faith is to cast a person of faith as someone who is less free, less reasonable, and even less human! This secular mindset often reduces the Church to a merely sociological entity stripped of its divine origin and mission. The Christian faith is mistakenly perceived as a set of abstract doctrines, moral restrictions, or pious sentimentality.

It is one thing for someone outside the Christian faith to hold such views. It is altogether another thing when those in our catechetical programs absorb this secular mindset toward faith and the Church. What invariably follows is that those we catechize may go through the motions of catechetical formation. But instead of deepening their convictions about faith they grow in indifference, apathy, hostility, and even rejection of the Gospel way of life with its beliefs, worship, and moral and spiritual life.

This pastoral reality is a particular challenge for catechists of the new evangelization. One catechetical approach in responding to this challenge is to present

Christian faith as a complete way of life. In the next chapter we will consider elements of an "***evangelizing catechesis***" that responds to this pastoral reality. Here we simply affirm the need for catechesis to present faith in Jesus Christ as the full human response to God's revelation transmitted through Sacred Scripture and Sacred Tradition. Catechesis in the new evangelization presents faith in Jesus Christ as a way of life that engages the entire human person — spirit, soul, mind, body, emotions, and will. This complete way of life engages the mind in understanding the truths of faith, the heart in conversion and living the Christian moral life, the will and the senses in the sacramental life of the Church, and the spirit in Christian prayer. Catechesis in the new evangelization includes the invitation to be formed in the "art of living" in the Church with the experience of faith as a complete way of life.

In this way the one being catechized is challenged to journey from the stance of disinterested observer, outside spectator, or critical judge, to an experience of total and living faith. As the *Catechism* teaches, "With his whole being man gives his assent to God the revealer … faith is a personal adherence of the whole man to God who reveals himself" (CCC 143, 176). This total adherence of the whole person is given to the Christian faith as professed in the Creed, celebrated in the Sacraments, lived in the Christian moral life, and deepened through prayer. Faith is thus presented as an all-encompassing way of life that fulfills the deepest desires of the human heart. And faith in Jesus Christ is lived as a personal reality that informs and transforms all aspects of human life. For as Pope Benedict has observed:

> Human life cannot be realized by itself. Our life is an open question, an incomplete project, still to be brought to fruition and realized. Each one's fundamental question is: How will this be realized — becoming man? How does one learn the art of living? Which is the path toward happiness?[29]

Catechists of the new evangelization remain alert to the spiritual longings and desires of those being catechized as the soil in which faith is planted and grows through catechesis, instruction, and faith formation. For the human search for the meaning and purpose of life remains, even when the actual experience of faith is obscured, diminished, or extinguished. The desire for happiness and the search for a life that is fully human endure as a necessary part of human experience. As the *Catechism* teaches, "The desire of God is written on the human heart, because man is created by God and for God; and God never ceases to draw man to himself. Only in God will he find the truth and happiness he never stops searching for."[30]

The Gospel teaches the "art of living" in the Church, and "Christ offers himself as the path of my life."[31] The concrete form that the "art of living" the Gospel takes was described by then Cardinal Joseph Ratzinger in this way:

> The *Sequela* (path) of Christ — Christ offers himself as the path of my life. (But) Sequela of Christ does not mean: imitating the man Jesus.

This type of attempt would necessarily fail…. The *Sequela* of Christ has a much higher goal: to be assimilated into Christ, that is to attain union with God. Such a word might sound strange to the ears of modern man. But, in truth, we all thirst for the infinite; for an infinite freedom, for happiness without limits … the *Sequela* of Christ is participation in the Cross, uniting oneself to his love, to the transformation of our life, which becomes the birth of the new man … whoever omits the Cross, omits the essence of Christianity.[32]

Catechesis in the new evangelization points to and forms others in a complete way of life that is the *Sequela Christi*, the "art of living" a new life in Jesus Christ. This "art of living" is inseparable from the Church's life. It encapsulates the Catholic faith as a way of life that includes beliefs, Sacraments, the moral and spiritual life. Catechists help those in catechetical formation to overcome the tendency to com-partmentalize or reduce faith to one or another of these dimensions. The catechist's ability to connect catechetical content with the "art of living" a Christian way of life shapes the catechetical effectiveness of the transmission of faith. For as Pope Benedict has noted:

To evangelize means: to show this path — to teach the art of living. At the beginning of his public life Jesus says: "I have come to evangelize the poor" (Luke 4:18); this means, I have the response to your fundamental question; I will show you the path of life, the path toward happiness — rather: I am the path…. This is why we are in need of a new evangeliza-tion — if the art of living remains an unknown, nothing else works. But this art is not the object of a science — this art can only be communi-cated by (one) who has life — he who is the Gospel personified. [33]

As a catechist presents the Gospel way of life that follows Jesus' path of the Cross and resurrection, the Gospel message is offered as a response to the deepest longings of the human heart and the search for happiness. Jesus' entire life, his sav-ing death, and glorious resurrection is proposed by the Church and by catechists as the "art of living" a fully human life in God.

The content of catechetical formation is drawn from the "deposit of faith," revealed in Sacred Scripture and Sacred Tradition, and presented in the *Catechism of the Catholic Church*. This content of catechesis, however, is not a set of abstract propositions. It always finds concrete expression in one or another dimension of the Christian way of life. Every article of faith on every page of the *Catechism of the Catholic Church*, reflects and is embodied in the "art of living" in the Church, the path of the Christian life. A catechist offers the full content of faith as an invitation to learn and to experience the "art of living" in Christ within the Church. In this way, faith is received as an answer to the fundamental search for life's meaning and purpose. For, "evangelizing is not merely a way of speaking, but a form of living: living in the listening and giving voice to the Father." [34]

A catechist may reflect on these questions: "How am I continually formed in the 'art of living' a new life in Christ?" "How does the catechetical formation I offer to others show the 'art of living' a new life in Christ within the Church?"

_____

_____

_____

_____

5. Catechesis in the new evangelization invites others into the "culture of the Church," through the heart of human culture transformed by grace.

The "art of living" in the Church represents a distinct Christian culture, understood as the Christian way of being fully human. This is important for catechetical ministry in the new evangelization since catechesis does not take place in a vacuum. Rather culture, as the network of human relationships, is the vital context in which catechesis is presented and received. Catechesis in the new evangelization makes possible the dramatic encounter between the culture of the Church and human culture, with all of its possibilities and limitations. In this way, the "new evangelization" means to promote a culture more deeply grounded in the Gospel and to discover the new man who is in us through the Spirit given us by Jesus Christ and the Father."[35] Here we encounter the "newness" of the "new evangelization," that is:

> Jesus Christ shows us how "the art of living" is learned "in an intense relationship with him. Through his love, Jesus Christ attracts to himself the people of every generation: in every age he convokes the Church, entrusting her with the proclamation of the Gospel by a mandate that is ever new. Today, there is a need for stronger ecclesial commitment to new evangelization in order to rediscover the joy of believing and the enthusiasm for communicating the faith.
>
> Note with Pastoral Recommendations for the Year of Faith, Congregation for the Doctrine of the Faith, January 6, 2012

> "New" not in its content but in its inner thrust, open to the grace of the Holy Spirit which constitutes the force of the new law of the Gospel that always renews the Church; "new" in ways that correspond with the power of the Holy Spirit and which are suited to the times and situations; "new" because of being necessary even in countries that have already received the proclamation of the Gospel.[36]

The image of a cathedral, with which we began this reflection, offers another insight into this dimension of catechesis in the new evangelization. For it can be said that in entering into a cathedral one moves into a sacred space, an apt metaphor for the living culture of the Church. But how is this interior space made sacred? How is the cathedral sanctified for the worship of God?

God's initiative and saving presence vivifies the Church's inner life or culture. In other words, it is always grace, understood as God's saving action and presence, which sanctifies the life of faith in every age and place. The interior of the cathedral building, no matter how beautifully designed and adorned, is neutral. It awaits and depends on the sanctifying action of a loving God who, by the power of the Holy Spirit, seeks our friendship through the living presence of His Son among His people. The Church is sanctified by God's living presence made real in the proclamation of the Word and in the Eucharistic mystery of the Body and Blood of Christ. The liturgical words and gestures of the priest, acting in the person of Jesus Christ, the High Priest, and the liturgical responses of the people of God who give praise and adoration, worship and thanksgiving, together sanctify the interior space as well. But it is God's loving initiative and ongoing activity and presence, through the power of the Holy Spirit, that makes holy, both priest and people. To enter into the "culture of the Church" through faith formation is to experience this power and sanctifying love of God.

Broadly understood, culture is the whole realm of human existence with its immense achievements, advances, and possibilities. Culture is the arena of human relationships and community. But it is also the place where human sinfulness, confusion, division, and violence deeply affect individuals in their relationships and in their communities. Blessed Pope John Paul II once described the reality of culture in this way:

> Culture is an expression of man, a confirmation of humanity. Man creates culture and through culture creates himself. He creates himself with the inward effort of the spirit, of thought, will and heart. At the same time he creates culture in communion with others. Culture is an expression of communication, of shared thought and collaboration by human beings. It is born of service of the common good and becomes an essential good of human communities.[37]

Human beings are both creators and recipients of culture, understood as the organic network of relationships and particular ways of life. And every person who receives catechetical formation from the Church receives at the same time a distinct Christian way of life inspired by the message of the Gospel. At times, this Christian way of life echoes and confirms the best and highest aspirations and achievements of the surrounding culture. At other times, the Gospel way of life runs counter to culture in its core values and messages.

Catechists of the new evangelization are aware of the profound effects of human sinfulness on contemporary culture. Any doubts about the reality and effects of sin on every aspect of human culture are overcome by simply reading or watching the daily news. Catechists know well that the surrounding culture shapes profoundly the catechetical context since both catechist and the one being catechized are formed by the culture that they shape and are shaped by.

The cultural context of catechesis is marked by tremendous possibility and deep ambiguity, by radiant light and profound darkness. With its apparently endless potential and its seemingly insurmountable challenges, culture is the necessary context for catechesis in the new evangelization. A catechist facilitates an encounter between the Gospel and the prevailing culture of the times, in its positive and negative dimensions.

Before a catechist invites others into the "culture of the Church," he or she takes time to reflect on the elements of human culture that both conform to and run counter to the Gospel. This reflection on culture is a necessary stage in effective catechetical ministry for the new evangelization. A catechist asks these vital questions: "What truth(s) of Christian faith sheds light on this cultural issue, problem, or challenge?" "What aspects of human culture resound with the Gospel?"

These reflections make possible an "*inculturated catechesis*," that leads those being catechized into the "culture of the Church," through the heart of human culture transformed by grace. The catechist assumes and searches for those elements of culture that are both in keeping with and contradict the Gospel message. Such reflection is a vital part of preparing for each catechetical session, as a catechist reflects on how the Gospel of Jesus Christ and the "art of living" in the Church find both resonance and resistance in culture.

A catechist encounters the values and messages of American culture in a variety of ways. The fact of being born, raised, formed, and educated in a particular culture is the most personal way in which we encounter, and are shaped by, its dominant values and messages. This formative influence of culture influences our common assumptions and informs our relationships, thoughts, decisions, and ways of life. The values and assumptions of contemporary culture impact a catechist in his or her catechetical ministry in ways that are conscious and unconscious, subtle and not so subtle. A catechist's daily conversion of life is deepened by reflection on the many ways in which the Gospel illumines or purifies our most basic cultural assumptions.

Catechists also encounter the values and messages of culture through the human interaction and dialogue that takes place within each catechetical moment. As catechists we know these catechetical moments well. Questions, challenges, indifference, and even resistance on the part of those we catechize can become profound "teaching moments," graced opportunities, when a catechist facilitates an encounter of the Gospel way of life with the ways of life offered by contemporary culture. Think of a moment when you, as a catechist, faced a difficult question, challenge, or plain indifference to catechetical formation that reflected common cultural assumptions. In these moments it is easy to react quickly or to become discouraged. It is also tempting to move to one of two extremes — on the one hand we can become harshly critical and constantly dismissive of contemporary culture without reflection on cultural elements that find resonance with the Gospel. On the other hand we can become overly accommodating to contemporary culture in a way that fails to critically discern its limitations and its need for purification in light of the Gospel. In a later chapter we will discuss some principles and pastoral approaches for an effective "*inculturated catechesis*." Here we simply acknowledge the task and the challenge for catechists in the new evangelization: to help those we catechize to enter more fully into the culture of the Gospel, or Gospel way of life, through the heart of human culture transformed by grace. A catechist may pose this question for reflection: "What are some common cultural assumptions that have shaped me and that I bring to my catechetical ministry?" "How do I respond, as a catechist, to questions, challenges, indifference, and even rejection, from those I have the privilege to form in faith?"

The revelation of the fundamental truths about God, about the human person and the world, is a great good for every human person, while living in darkness without the truths about ultimate questions is an evil … this is why Saint Paul did not hesitate to describe conversion to the Christian faith as liberation "from the power of darkness," and entrance into "the kingdom of his beloved Son in whom we have redemption and the forgiveness of our sins" (Col 1:13–14).

Congregation for the Doctrine of the Faith, *Doctrinal Note on Some Aspects of Evangelization*, December 2007

Opening the door of faith

So far we have considered Trinitarian, Christological, ecclesial, and cultural dimensions of catechesis in the new evangelization. These reflections, drawn from the image of entering into a cathedral, lead us to consider how catechists might engage in an *evangelizing* catechesis and an *inculturated* catechesis that serves the new evangelization. These considerations will be the focus of the following chapters.

In reflecting on the catechetical dimensions of the new evangelization we are reminded of the need for patience, humility, and Christian hope. These particular virtues, that should mark the life and ministry of a catechist, have been described by Pope Benedict XVI in these words:

Yet another temptation lies hidden beneath this — the temptation of impatience, the temptation of immediately finding great success, in finding large numbers. But this is not God's way. For the Kingdom of God as well as for evangelization, the instrument and vehicle of the Kingdom of God, the parable of the grain of mustard seed is always valid (Mark 4:31–32). New evangelization cannot mean: immediately attracting the large masses that have distanced themselves from the Church by using new and more refined methods. No — this is not what new evangelization promises. New evangelization means: never being satisfied with the fact that from the grain of mustard seed, the great tree of the Universal Church grew … the new evangelization must surrender to the mystery of the grain of mustard seed and not be so pretentious as to believe to immediately produce a large tree. We either live too much in the security of the already existing large tree or in the impatience of having a greater, more vital tree — instead, we must accept the mystery that the Church is at the same time a large tree and a very small grain. [38]

Let us return to the image of entering a cathedral as we bring this chapter to a close. In considering elements of catechesis that serve the new evangelization we are led to ask: "What do people expect in catechetical formation once they enter the door of faith?" "How might the catechetical formation we offer open the door of faith to the Gospel way of life that is appropriated as a fully Christian and fully human life?" Or to put it in imaginative terms, "Why should anyone journey, through the church doors, from mere observation or admiration of a cathedral into the interior cathedral space where the beauty and splendor of faith is revealed?" These questions draw us to reflect on the Church's permanent task of evangelization that will be reviewed in brief in the next chapter. Then we will consider some principles and pastoral approaches for an "evangelizing catechesis."

To conclude, our reflections so far on catechetical challenges in the new evangelization lead catechists to return their gaze to Jesus Christ, the door through which all the baptized pass into the community of the Church. And it is in the Church that catechists and those they are privileged to form are shaped in the "art of living" in Christ in faith, hope and love. As Blessed Pope John Paul II noted in a homily given during one of his pastoral visits to the United States of America:

> In the Gospel Jesus says: "I am the door, whoever enters through me will be saved, and will come in and go out and find pasture" (John 10:9). Our Christian life can be seen as a great pilgrimage to the house of the Father, which passes through the door that is Jesus Christ. The key to that door is repentance and conversion. The strength to pass through that door comes from our faith and hope and love. For many Catholics, an important part of the journey must be to rediscover the joy of belonging to the Church, to *cherish the Church* as the Lord has given her to us, as *Mother and Teacher*. [39]

Questions for Reflection and Discussion

1. Share one fresh insight into your catechetical ministry and the new evangelization from your reflection on Pope Benedict XVI's image of entering a cathedral.

2. Identify concrete ways in which the catechetical formation you offer invites others to an experience of God's grace in and through the person of Jesus Christ?

_____

_____

3. How often do you give personal witness to your Catholic faith in your role as a catechist?

_____

_____

4. Identify those catechetical moments that can be graced opportunities for your personal witness to faith?

_____

_____

5. Do you experience faith as a complete way of life, as the "art of living" in the Church? Identify ways you can begin to invite those you catechize to a personal encounter with Jesus Christ, who is the path of Christian living.

_____

_____

6. What common cultural assumptions and values shape and impact your catechetical ministry? What common cultural assumptions and values shape and impact the lives of those you are privileged to form in faith through catechetical ministry?

_____

_____

CHAPTER TWO

Proposing
the Gospel Anew
Toward an
"Evangelizing Catechesis"

We have just considered various catechetical dimensions of the new evangelization evoked by the image of entering into a cathedral. We may summarize these reflections in this way:

- The reality of God's divine initiative of grace is a starting point for catechesis in the new evangelization. A catechist has the privileged task of extending this divine invitation in the various moments of faith formation. To open hearts and minds to the mystery of divine grace is an essential moment in effective faith formation in the new evangelization. For catechesis that begins and ends with divine grace engages the common cultural assumption that one does not need divine grace to live a fully human life. A catechist leads others to awareness and acceptance of the offer of divine grace rather than self-sufficiency and alienation from God. In witnessing to God's love and grace, as a "mystery of light," that breaks into human experience, a catechist introduces others to a relationship with God who is revealed as Father, Son and Holy Spirit. The divine desire for communion and friendship with every human person is the basis for this proclamation of faith. God alone reveals himself to man, and God alone reveals man to himself. Catechesis in the new evangelization is always a "communication of the living mystery of God" (Blessed Pope John Paul II, *Catechesi Tradendae*, 7).

- Catechesis in the new evangelization centers on the person of Jesus Christ as the origin, the goal, and the measure of authentic faith formation. A catechist opens the door of faith to Jesus Christ, the One who leads us to the Father in the power of the Holy Spirit through the ministry of the Church. A catechist looks always to Christ who says, "I am the door; if anyone enters by me, he will be saved, and will go in and out and find pasture" (John 10:9). The effectiveness of catechesis in support of the new evangelization will depend on the extent to which a catechist places the Paschal Mystery of Christ's life, Cross, Death and Resurrection, at the center of all catechetical activities. To serve the new evangelization is to be committed to "transmitting not one's own teaching or that of some other master, but the teaching of Jesus Christ, the Truth that He communicates or, to put it more precisely, the Truth that He is."[40] Christ-centered faith formation is at the heart of a truly evangelizing catechesis.

- Catechesis in the new evangelization invites others to rediscover the joy of belonging to the Church, the visible instrument chosen by Christ to extend his saving and healing mission in the world. This ecclesial dimension of catechesis in the new evangelization is rooted in the catechist's ongoing personal conversion through full and active participation in the Church's life. The catechist's daily journey of interior conversion is sustained by the Holy Spirit, the "primary agent of evangelization." A catechist is committed to daily reading and contemplation of God's Word and frequent participation in the Sacraments that sanctify and strengthen by the power of the Holy Spirit. From such daily conversion of life flows a catechist's convictions and joy in the truths of faith, and his or her personal witness to the beauty and challenges of lived faith. The Gospel way of life, as summarized in the *Catechism of the Catholic Church*, is shared and received in each catechetical context as life-giving revealed truths received in faith, rather than as abstract theological propositions imposed by the Church. The truths of faith, presented in the *Catechism,* are conveyed, through appropriate catechetical methodologies, as expressions of the lived experience of new life in Jesus Christ.

> Whatever be the level of his responsibility in the Church, every catechist must constantly endeavor to transmit by his teaching and behavior the teaching and life of Jesus. He will not seek to keep directed towards himself and his personal opinions and attitudes the attention and consent of the mind and heart of the person he is catechizing. Above all, he will not try to inculcate his personal opinions and options as if they expressed Christ's teaching and the lessons of his life. Every catechist should be able to apply to himself the mysterious words of Jesus: "my teaching is not mine, but of Him who sent me." (John 7:16) … what assiduous study of God's word transmitted by the Church's Magisterium, what profound familiarity with Christ and with the Father, what a spirit of prayer, what detachment from self must a catechist have in order to say: "my teaching is not mine!"
>
> Blessed Pope John Paul II, *On Catechesis in Our Time*, 6

- Catechesis in the new evangelization draws with confidence and charity on the truths of faith summarized in the *Catechism of the Catholic Church*. The *Catechism* is the sure reference point and authoritative source for the content of faith formation. A catechist receives this content of faith in humility and with gratitude. The "success" of faith formation efforts in the new evangelization rests on the rediscovery of the *Catechism* as a vital catechetical tool.

- Catechesis in the new evangelization is attentive to the possibilities and challenges of American culture as the lived context in which catechesis takes place. Faith formation in the new evangelization does not take place in a void. Rather, culture with its values, assumptions, and worldviews is the soil in which the seed of faith is sown in hearts and minds. Both catechist and the one receiving catechetical formation shapes and is shaped by the surrounding culture. A catechist invites others to experience the "culture of the Church" through the heart of human culture transformed by grace. In the dialogue between faith and culture a catechist responds to doubts, indifference, and even rejection of Gospel truths in light of basic cultural assumptions, popular misperceptions, and negative stereotypes about Christian faith and the Catholic Church. Sustained reflection on the elements of human culture that both resound with and run counter to the Gospel is a necessary step in catechesis in the new evangelization.

The challenge of presenting an "evangelizing catechesis"

In describing the work of the Pontifical Council for the Promotion of the New Evangelization, Pope Benedict XVI has spoken of the need to "re-propose the Gospel anew" to people today. To "re-propose the Gospel" is also the duty and task of catechists, evangelists, and the lay faithful, as each takes their part in the new evangelization. As the Holy Father observed:

> Evangelization is not only the Church's living teaching, the first proclamation of the faith (kerygma) and instruction, formation in the faith (catechesis); it is also the *entire wide-ranging commitment to reflect on revealed truth.*
>
> Blessed Pope John Paul II, *Crossing the Threshold of Hope*, 107

> There are regions of the world that are still awaiting a first evangelization; others that have received it, but need a deeper intervention; yet others in which the Gospel put down roots a long time ago, giving rise to a true Christian tradition but in which, in recent centuries with complex dynamics the secularization process has produced a serious crisis of the meaning of the Christian faith and of belonging to the Church. From this perspective, I have decided to create a new body, in the form of a "Pontifical Council," whose principal task will be to promote a renewed evangelization in the countries where the first proclamation of the faith has already resonated and where Churches with an ancient foundation exist but are experiencing a progressive secularization of society … which pose a challenge to finding appropriate ways to propose anew the perennial truth of Christ's Gospel. [41]

What does it mean to "re-propose the Gospel"? How is a catechist to effectively "re-propose" anew the life-giving truths of the Gospel to those shaped by a secularizing culture? How does the re-proposing of the Gospel reflect the distinct goals and aims of evangelization and catechesis? And finally, what are some catechetical principles and pastoral approaches to guide the "re-proposing of the Gospel" in a given time and place? These are some of the catechetical challenges in the new evangelization that this chapter will focus on. Discussion questions to guide group or personal reflections are offered at the end of this chapter.

Evangelization and catechesis: a dynamic relationship

To effectively "re-propose the Gospel," evangelists, catechists, and the faithful are to present what we may call an "*evangelizing catechesis*." They do so without confusing the Church's ministries of evangelization and catechesis. Instead, through an "*evangelizing catechesis*" a catechist takes seriously the distinct demands of both evangelization and catechesis while respecting each as a unique moment in the Church's ministry of the word. Above all, an "*evangelizing catechesis*" aims to open the door of faith and invite others onto the path of conversion to the person of Jesus Christ, so that faith matures and deepens into lifelong discipleship.

> All Christians are called to this witness, and in this way they can be real evangelizers.
>
> Pope Paul VI, *Evangelii Nuntiandi*, 21

Responding to the need for an "evangelizing catechesis"

Pause for a moment to reflect on a pastoral reality that you, as a catechist, have most likely encountered during your weekly catechetical sessions. It is the pastoral situation in which those you catechize may also happen to be those who have not received and accepted in faith the basic message of the Gospel. This may, at first, sound like an improbable or strange contradiction. In fact, it is a distinct catechetical challenge that catechists and teachers face each day and week in the classroom and in catechetical settings. It is the particular challenge of catechizing those who have yet to be evangelized.

In the pastoral scenario described above, a catechist is offering ongoing faith formation to a person who has not yet experienced personal conversion to Jesus Christ as the Way, the Truth, and the Life. The result is that he or she may go through the motions of catechetical formation and sacramental preparation without being evangelized into the "culture of the Church," as the total way of the Christian life. Catechetical preparation for the Sacraments of Initiation — Baptism, Confirmation and Eucharist — become "catechetical hoops" for children, teens, and adults to jump through, rather than graced moments that initiate one into a relationship with the living God. Faith formation becomes an obstacle course to be completed rather than the door to active participation in the liturgical worship of the Church and in formation for lifelong Christian discipleship through daily conversion to Jesus Christ. There is a good chance that a Catholic child, teenager, or adult enrolled in a catechetical program who has not been evangelized will eventually join the ranks of "former Catholics," or "lapsed Catholics," or simply Catholics whose faith formation did not initiate or encourage a lifelong Christian discipleship. The

General Directory for Catechesis highlights this widespread pastoral challenge in this way:

> In pastoral practice it is not always easy to define the boundaries of these activities. Frequently, many who present themselves for catechesis truly require genuine conversion. Because of this the Church usually desires that the first stage in the catechetical process be dedicated to ensuring conversion. In the "mission *ad gentes*," this task is normally accomplished during the "pre-catechumenate." In the context of the "new evangelization" it is effected by means of a "kerygmatic catechesis," sometimes called "pre-catechesis," because it is based on the precatechumate and is proposed by the Gospel and directed towards a solid option of faith. Only by starting with conversion … can catechesis strictly speaking, fulfill its proper task of education in the faith.[42]

In those pastoral situations where those in faith formation stand in need of genuine conversion the catechetical moment itself needs to include evangelizing moments. An "***evangelizing catechesis,***" that re-proposes the Gospel, becomes a necessary and timely response to this pastoral reality. While evangelization and catechesis are not identical, they also are not disconnected aspects of faith formation. Rather, they are related, yet discrete moments in faith formation. To understand the elements of an *"evangelizing catechesis"* that invites conversion of life, let us consider first the distinct and complementary aims of evangelization and catechesis, as well as the essential relationship between these fundamental dimensions of the Church's missionary activity. A discussion on catechetical principles and appropriate pastoral approaches for an "***evangelizing catechesis***" that "re-proposes the Gospel" will follow.

Evangelization and catechesis: distinct yet complementary aspects of the new evangelization

As a catechist prepares to serve the new evangelization it is helpful at the outset to understand and reflect on the relationship between evangelization and catechesis. Such an understanding also helps those involved in faith formation to recognize that these two dimensions of the Church's mission do not stand in competition or in opposition to each other. Rather, each serves complementary dimensions of the Church's single proclamation of faith in Jesus Christ. Evangelists and catechists stand side by side, complementing, supporting, and encouraging each other in their distinct tasks and challenges. This is how the *General Directory for Catechesis* speaks of the complex, rich, and dynamic reality that is the "process of evangelization":

> The missionary mandate of Jesus to evangelize has various aspects, all of which, however, are closely connected with each other: "proclaim" (Mark 16:15), "make disciples and teach," "be my witnesses," "baptize," "do this in memory of me" (Luke 22:19), "love one another" (John

15:12). Proclamation, witness, teaching, sacraments, love of neighbor: all of these aspects are the means by which the one Gospel is transmitted and they constitute the essential elements of evangelization itself.[43]

These various elements of evangelization constitute the many ways in which the Church is built up in every time and place, namely through Christian witness and proclamation, Word and Sacrament, interior conversion and social transformation, and the catechumenate and Christian initiation. We may highlight these "essential but different moments" in the process of evangelization: "missionary activity directed towards non-believers and those who live in religious indifference; initial catechetical activity for those who choose the Gospel and for those who need to complete or modify their initiation; pastoral activity directed toward the Christian faithful of mature faith in the Christian community" (*General Directory for Catechesis*, 49).

A "primary or first proclamation" of the basic Gospel message is aimed at non-believers and to those living in religious indifference or apathy. In this moment of evangelization a person encounters the Gospel message of faith in Jesus Christ and is invited to accept that life-giving message through ongoing conversion in light of God's word and through participation in the Church's sacramental life.

The *General Directory for Catechesis* describes this pastoral situation in this way:

In many countries of established Christian tradition and sometimes in younger Churches there exists "an intermediate situation," where "entire groups of the baptized have lost a living sense of the faith, or even no longer consider themselves members of the Church and live a life far removed from Christ and his Gospel." Such situations require "a new evangelization" … here primary proclamation and basic catechesis are priorities. [44]

Catechesis is distinct from this primary proclamation of the Gospel. Yet catechesis depends on evangelization even as it promotes and matures the initial moment of conversion. A catechist welcomes the one who is converted to the Gospel and incorporates him into the Christian community through ongoing faith formation. In the words of Blessed Pope John Paul II:

The specific aim of catechesis is to develop, with God's help, an as yet initial faith, and to advance in fullness and to nourish day by day the Christian life of the faithful, young and old. It is in fact a matter of giving growth, at the level of knowledge and in life, to the seed of faith sown by the Holy Spirit with the initial proclamation and effectively transmitted by Baptism … to put it more precisely: within the whole process of evangelization, the aim of catechesis is to be the teaching and maturation stage, that is to say, the period in which the Christian, having accepted by faith the person of Jesus Christ as the one Lord and having given Him complete adherence by sincere conversion of heart, endeavors to know better this Jesus to whom he has entrusted himself, to know his "mystery," the kingdom of God proclaimed by Him, the requirements and promises contained in His Gospel message, and the paths that He has laid down for anyone who wishes to follow Him. [45]

Faith is matured and deepened through a catechist's systematic presentation of the profession of faith in the Creed, as summarized in the *Catechism of the Catholic Church*. The door of faith is opened through catechetical instruction and formation in the complete Christian way of life, nourished by the Sacraments, shaped by Christian moral precepts, and deepened in prayer. "In truth," says the *General Directory for Catechesis*, "the inner growth of the Church and her correspondence with God's plan depend essentially on catechesis. In this sense, catechesis must always be considered a priority in evangelization." [46]

Between evangelization and catechesis then there exists a "relationship of complementary distinction … both activities are essential and mutually complementary: go and welcome, proclaim and educate, call and incorporate." [47] This essential relationship between evangelization and catechesis has been described in this way:

> Catechesis is one of these moments — a very remarkable one — in the whole process of evangelization. That is to say that there are activities which "prepare" for catechesis and activities which "derive" from it. The "moment" of catechesis is that which corresponds to the period in which conversion to Jesus Christ is formalized, and provides a basis for first adhering to him. Converts, by means of "a period of formation, an apprenticeship in the whole Christian life," are initiated into the mystery of salvation and an evangelical style of life. This means "initiating the hearers into the fullness of the Christian life." [48]

An awareness of the complementary yet distinct tasks of evangelists and catechists is vital to effective catechesis in the new evangelization. Evangelists sow the seeds of faith by calling forth conversion of heart and mind and lifelong discipleship to the person of Jesus Christ. Catechists nurture and bring to bloom the seeds of faith through systematic faith formation, instruction that transmits faithfully the content of faith, and personal witness to the fullness and joy of the Christian life lived in the community of the Church.

In pastoral situations where those being catechized stand in need of evangelization, a catechist is attentive to call forth conversion of life and commitment to personal discipleship to Jesus Christ, at strategic points in each catechetical session. Both catechist and the one being catechized return, time and time again, to the fundamentals of the Gospel message — God's love and the divine initiative of grace, divine Revelation that reaches its fullness in the Incarnation of God in the person of Jesus Christ, the sacramental life and ministry of the Church as the visible continuation of Christ's saving mission, and the Christian moral life as the lived expression of love for God and neighbor.

In this way a catechist responds to the particular pastoral challenge in which, "frequently people who come for catechesis need to live more truly converted lives.

Therefore, programs of catechesis and introduction to the faith might benefit from putting greater emphasis on the proclamation of the Gospel, which is a call to this conversion and which fosters and sustains it. In this way, the new evangelization can reinvigorate the present programs of instruction in the faith by accentuating the kerygmatic character of proclamation." [49] Through such an "*evangelizing catechesis*" the catechetical moment itself includes a "re-proposing of the Gospel."

The catechetical challenge of "re-proposing the Gospel"

In each catechetical session, teachers and catechists are presented with multiple opportunities to re-propose the basic message of the Gospel. However, those involved in faith formation know well the challenges that come with their catechetical activities. A catechist is often limited by the time constraints of a given catechetical or religious education curriculum. The difficulty of identifying convenient times for faith formation given the hectic pace of everyday life and the over committed schedules of parishioners, the influence of pervasive secular values that are contrary to the Gospel, and a general indifference and apathy toward religious faith, are only some of the real challenges that catechists and teachers face each day. In addition, various catechetical audiences: baptized Catholics in sacramental preparation programs, baptized Catholics in ongoing faith formation programs, baptized Catholics who no longer actively practice the faith, and those seeking to enter into the full communion of the Church — each have distinct pedagogical and methodological needs that a catechist carefully and prayerfully considers.

What does it mean then for a catechist or an evangelist to "propose faith"? What are some key elements that a catechist considers in "re-proposing the Gospel" today? To help us understand the act of proposing the faith of the Church we turn to reflect on the ordinary human experience of making or receiving a proposal. We do so assuming that there are elements in the human experience of offering or receiving a proposal that might shed light on the ecclesial and catechetical act of proposing the Gospel. From this reflection we may highlight some principles and pastoral approaches to the catechetical task of "re-proposing the Gospel" today.

Proposing the Gospel today

Daily human interactions abound with examples of offering and receiving proposals.

In the commercial realm, the daily exchange of material goods involves proposing and accepting products, in terms of their quality and appeal. The whole range of commercial advertizing and marketing is based on proposing the benefits of products to a potential customer. Every time you purchase a product you implicitly accept the manufacturer's proposal as to its benefits, value, and worth.

In the realm of human relationships, offering and accepting proposals is also part of everyday life. In the raising of their children parents continually propose to their children Christian virtues as paths of thought and action. A teacher proposes to his or her student certain ways of thinking and understanding while instilling a lifelong love for learning. In the Sunday homily, a pastor proposes the revealed Word of God as a guide on the path of daily Christian discipleship.

There is one instance of the human experience of offering and receiving a proposal that we might consider more closely. It is the proposal offered by a man to a woman, as they together prepare to enter into the covenant of marriage. This human experience of offering and receiving a proposal could provide some experiential insight into the ecclesial act of "proposing anew the Gospel" in the new evangelization.

A proposal of marriage is offered within the context of the experience of human love as self-gift. The offer of a marriage proposal is rooted in the order of love and freedom, the very opposite of the order of power and self-seeking. The vocation to marriage as the union of one man and one woman provides the larger framework for a proposal of marriage. Within that larger context, the couple's friendship, mutual attraction, trust, and shared interests provides the lived background that is unique to their relationship. A proposal of marriage from a complete stranger who has no personal or family connections, or who is completely unknown, would be a contradiction in terms. The context of the couple's relationship of friendship and love assures the genuineness of the proposal, while the mutual freedom of both persons guarantees its soundness and strength. The man is completely free in offering his proposal of marriage and the woman is completely free in accepting his proposal. What is proposed is nothing less than a shared and lasting life together, a communion of life and love that will be nurtured and sustained by mutual self-giving and trust. The man entrusts himself and his future life to the woman's love. In return he receives the entrusting of her life and love as she freely receives and accepts his proposal. The proposal of love, once accepted, will continue to be offered and accepted again and again as the love of the spouses for each other and for their children unfolds within the stable and faithful communion of marriage and family life. Freedom, friendship, trust, and self giving love all find concrete expression in the human experience of a proposal of marriage.

Like any example from human experience, this too is limited in its application. However, this human experience provides some insight into the elements of the act of re-proposing the Gospel message to advance the new evangelization. For one, the catechist's act of proposing the Gospel is rooted primarily in the order of God's love and our human freedom to accept or decline the divine offer of love. The vocation of each human person to friendship with God is the broader context for any proposal of the Gospel message. The Church, as the Body of Christ, and each local community of believers forms the lived context in which the Gospel message is proposed. This living faith of the Christian community is the necessary experiential framework for the offer of any proposal of faith in Jesus Christ.

In each catechetical setting the personal experience of mutual trust, openness, and genuine human friendships serves as the backdrop against which the re-proposing of the Gospel takes place. A catechist creates and engages in a dialogue of personal friendship and self giving love, while inviting others to consider and accept the proposal to live as a full member of the community of disciples in Jesus Christ. This personal dynamic of evangelization and catechesis has been described in this way:

> Evangelization also involves a sincere dialogue that seeks to understand the reasons and feelings of others. Indeed, the heart of another person can only be approached in freedom, in love and in dialogue, in such a manner that the word which is spoken is not simply offered, but also truly witnessed in the hearts of those to whom it is addressed. This requires taking into account the hopes, sufferings and concrete situations of those with whom one is in dialogue. Precisely in this way, people of good will open their hearts more freely and share their spiritual and religious experiences in all sincerity. This experience of sharing, a characteristic of true friendship, is a valuable occasion for witnessing and for Christian proclamation.[50]

An "evangelizing catechesis" — principles and practical approaches

The human experience of offering and receiving a proposal provides insight into the ecclesial act of "proposing anew the Gospel" in the new evangelization. From these experiential elements we may draw principles and pastoral approaches that mark an "evangelizing catechesis."

- A catechist seeks to re-propose the Gospel anew in the conviction that every "man is by nature and vocation a religious being. Coming from God, going toward God, man lives a fully human life only if he freely lives by his bond with God" (CCC 44). A catechist's confidence in offering an "evangelizing catechesis" is rooted in the conviction that in every child, youth, and adult, "there is a deeper hunger that only God can satisfy. Human beings of the third millennium want an authentic, full life; they need truth, profound freedom, love freely given. Even in the deserts of the secularized world, man's soul thirsts for God, for the living God." [51]

- A truly "evangelizing catechesis" is permeated by the "law of love." The *Catechism of the Catholic Church* highlights the primacy of love in catechesis when it notes that, "the whole concern of doctrine and its teachings must be directed to the love that never ends" (CCC 25). The inspiration, motivation, and guiding principle of the ministry of every evangelist and catechist is the "law of love," rooted in the love of God revealed in Jesus Christ. This witness to Christian love takes primary place in the "re-proposing of the Gospel" in the new evangelization.

In providing faith formation and catechetical instruction to children, youth, and adults, the catechist understands that it is not a matter of winning an argument, or showcasing one's superior knowledge of the faith or theological expertise. It is still less an opportunity to draw attention to one's own cleverness or eloquence in presenting the faith of the Church. Instead the catechist engages in what has been called an "apologetics of love,"[52] that points to both the reasonableness and the beauty of the Gospel proclaimed, believed, and lived in the Church. The personal witness to and example of Christian love is a compelling force beyond a catechist's words. For this personal witness to love gives evidence of faith that has transformed one's own life, and therefore has the graced capacity to transform the life of the one being catechized.

The priority and impetus of love in the new evangelization flow from the Paschal Mystery of Jesus' life, death and Resurrection. As Christ reveals the love and saving plan of the Father in the mystery of his life, his death and his Resurrection, the catechist in turn reveals that divine love to the one being evangelized and catechized. In doing so, the catechist's love for Christ, the Church, and for the one being catechized, serves as a convincing and concrete witness to divine love.

Catechesis in the new evangelization finds its deepest roots in that love that alone is the way of divine revelation, the love of God that alone is ultimately and intrinsically credible. Since God chose the way of love as the means to reveal himself and his plan for the world's redemption, catechetical efforts to propose the Gospel anew follow in the same way of divine love. The "divine pedagogy" of love shapes and informs a catechist's pedagogy of love. The authority and certainty of Sacred Scripture and Sacred Tradition also rests on the revealing love of God. In this way, a fresh proposing of the Gospel through an *"evangelizing catechesis"* originates and ends in the love of God revealed to each human person. This primacy of love in all faith formation activities in the new evangelization is summarized in these words:

> The primary motive of evangelization is the love of Christ for the eternal salvation of all. The sole desire of authentic evangelizers is to bestow freely what they themselves have freely received … the mission of the Apostles and its continuation in the mission of the early Church remain the foundational model of evangelization for all time … before all the world, they display an unarmed strength brimming with love for all people … indeed, love impels the followers of Christ to proclaim to all the truth which saves. Such love is the sign of the authentic presence of the Holy Spirit who, as the principal agent of evangelization, never ceases to move people's hearts when they hear the Gospel, by opening them to receive it. It is a love which lives in the heart of the Church and from there, as burning charity radiates out to the ends of the earth, as far as the heart of every human being. The entire heart of man awaits the encounter with Jesus Christ.[53]

- An "evangelizing catechesis" draws on the content of the *Catechism* to open the door of faith particularly to those for whom faith has lost its savor and value. In re-proposing the Gospel message a catechist is challenged to answer questions that speak not only to the *what?* of the Catholic faith, but also to the *"why?"* of Catholic faith (its reasonableness and intelligibility), and the *"so what?"* (the relevance and life transforming power of Christian faith). In this way, a re-proposing of the Gospel aims to instruct and form others in the fundamentals of Christian faith, to show the reasonableness of faith, to inspire renewed awe before the mysteries of faith, and to "cultivate delight," as Saint Augustine puts it, in the life-changing power of the Gospel.

  The catechist, like a museum docent who points to the beauty of an artistic masterpiece, presents the Gospel way of life as attractive. Christian faith is proposed as the most authentic and attractive way to live a fully human life in God and in the community of the Church, and therefore worthy of entrusting one's entire life. A person who is compelled by the beauty and reasonableness of Christian faith will be opened to its truth. As the Second Vatican Council teaches, "truth can impose itself on the mind only in virtue of its own truth, which wins over the mind with both gentleness and power." [54] An *"evangelizing catechesis"* is grounded in the reality that the acceptance of a proposal of the Gospel message is to encounter ultimately a Person, the Person of Jesus Christ, whose divine love and whose truth sets us free and wins over the heart and mind.

- Finally, the virtue of humility marks a catechist's presentation of an *"evangelizing catechesis"* that proposes the Gospel anew. The Christian virtue of humility flows from genuine Christian love. The practice of humility, as a mark of a catechist, imitates the example of Jesus himself. Humility also reflects the "divine pedagogy" of God who out of love for the world sent his only Son into the world, so that we might live through Him (1 John 4:9). As Saint Paul writes in his hymn to the Incarnation: "Christ Jesus, who, though he was in the form of God, did not count equality with God something to be grasped, but emptied himself, taking the form of a servant, being born in the likeness of men. And being found in human form he humbled himself and became obedient unto death, even death on a cross" (Philippians 2:5–8).

  The exercise of humility in catechetical activities allows a catechist to recognize when to clearly and lovingly re-propose the Gospel message and when to step back and to allow God's love revealed in Jesus Christ to speak to the heart and mind of a person. In speaking of appropriate methods in the new evangelization, then Cardinal Joseph Ratzinger pointed to this principle of "expropriation of one's person," in humility and in love, when he said:

The correct method derives from this structure of the new evangelization. Of course, we must use the modern methods of making ourselves be heard in a reasonable way — or better yet, of making the voice of the Lord accessible and comprehensible … we are not looking for listening for ourselves — we do not want to increase the power and the spreading of our institutions, but we wish to serve the good of the people and humanity giving room to He who is Life … this expropriation of one's person, offering it to Christ for the salvation of men, is the fundamental condition of true commitment for the Gospel … the Trinitarian plan — visible in the Son, who does not speak in his name — shows the form of life of the true evangelizer — rather, evangelizing is not merely a way of speaking, but a form of living: living in the listening and giving voice to the Father. [55]

Questions for Reflection and Discussion

1. How have you, as a catechist, experienced the fruits of the Church's permanent evangelizing mission? Reflect on how the call you received to serve the Church as a catechist was nourished and continues to be strengthened by the Church's "permanent evangelization."

2. How do you respond to the pastoral challenge of catechizing those who have not yet been evangelized to the basic message of the Gospel? Discuss how the approach presented in this chapter support you in responding to this particular catechetical challenge.

3. Discuss the relationship between evangelization and catechesis as complementary activities that serve the Church's essential missionary nature and identity.

4. Discuss how you understand the task of "proposing the Gospel anew" to those you form in the faith. Identify obstacles you face in proposing the message of the Gospel today and how you respond to them in light of the principles and approaches discussed in this chapter.

_____

_____

CHAPTER THREE

BRIDGING FAITH AND CULTURE — TOWARD AN "INCULTURATED CATECHESIS"

> The inherent missionary nature of the Church means testifying essentially to the fact that the task of inculturation, as an integral dissemination of the Gospel and its consequent translation into thought and life, continues today, and represents the heart, the means, and the goal of the new evangelization. [56]

These words of Blessed Pope John Paul II highlight the *inculturation* of the Gospel as the heart and goal of the new evangelization. We are reminded that an essential element of effective catechesis is the inculturation of the Gospel in the lives of those being evangelized and catechized. It could be said that catechists of the new evangelization are challenged to present an "***inculturated catechesis.***"

In the last chapter we considered various dimensions of an "***evangelizing catechesis.***" In this chapter, we turn to focus on principles and pastoral approaches for an "***inculturated catechesis***" that supports the new evangelization. We will draw on an example from the world of art — a series of paintings by the French impressionist Claude Monet — as an image for the essential catechetical task of bridging faith and culture. We will highlight virtues that guide a catechist to inculturate the Gospel. And we will consider four cultural challenges to catechesis, namely, secularization, individualism, relativism, and the dominant media culture. Practical ways you can respond to these cultural challenges will also be discussed.

To guide our reflections in this chapter we begin by considering the following questions: Why inculturate the Gospel? What concrete forms does an "inculturated catechesis" take today? Why is reflection on the relationship of the Gospel to culture an essential aspect of a catechist's own formation and preparation for each catechetical session? And how might our catechetical and faith formation programs become "centers of inculturation" in the new evangelization?

Inculturation of the Gospel in catechesis for the new evangelization

The Church's perennial evangelization, rooted in Jesus' command to "go and make disciples of all nations," finds concrete expression in the inculturation of the Gospel in every place and age. We go back in time to the birth of the Church at Pentecost, described in the second chapter of the Book of Acts. There we read the dramatic account of the coming of the Holy Spirit on the Church:

> When the day of Pentecost had come, they were all together in one place. And suddenly a sound came from heaven like the rush of a mighty wind, and it filled all the house where they were sitting. And there appeared tongues as of fire, distributed and resting on each one of them. And they were all filled with the Holy Spirit and began to speak in other tongues, as the Spirit gave them utterance. (Acts 2:1–4)

Immediately after the descent of the Holy Spirit on the apostles, the first inculturation of the Gospel follows. For as soon as the apostles receive the Holy Spirit they begin to speak in other languages, "as the Spirit gave them utterance," proclaiming the Good News of faith in Jesus Christ and the mighty works of God. People who had gathered there from diverse cultures and languages heard and understood the apostles in their own languages. We are told that, "the multitude came together and they were bewildered, because each one heard them speaking in his own language. And they were amazed saying, 'Are not all these who are speaking Galileans? And how is it that we hear, each of us, in his own native language?... We hear them telling in our own tongues the mighty works of God.' And all were amazed and perplexed, saying to one another, 'What does this mean?'" (Acts 2:6–12).

The account of Pentecost reminds us that the inculturation of Christian faith, through evangelization and catechesis is, first and foremost, a gift and work of the Holy Spirit. Just as the unity of the Church at Pentecost is a work of the Holy Spirit, so too is the inculturation of the Gospel a work of the Holy Spirit. This inculturation of Christian faith is more than a simple translation of the Gospel proclamation into another language. It involves the transformation of cultural criteria, modes of thought, and lifestyles in the power of the Holy Spirit and in the light of the Gospel. Whenever evangelists and catechists inculturate the Gospel they extend into every time, place, and culture the moment and the grace of Pentecost.

In the faith-culture dialogue there is a two-fold movement that a catechist considers and applies to each catechetical moment: "In this work of inculturation, the Christian community must discern, on the one hand, which riches to 'take' up as compatible with the faith; on the other, it must seek to 'purify' and 'transform' those criteria, modes of thought and lifestyles that are contrary to the Kingdom of God. Such discernment is governed by two basic principles: 'compatibility with the Gospel and communion with the universal Church.' All of the people of God need to be involved in this process ... in such a way that it really is an expression of the community's Christian experience." [57] This two-fold movement leads us to identify key theological and catechetical principles for the inculturation of faith. In doing so, we begin with the question — why inculturate the Gospel?

The mystery of the Incarnation — the "original" inculturation of the Word of God

A first reason for the inculturation of the Gospel is the central Christian mystery of faith — the Incarnation of God in the person of Jesus Christ. For "the Word of God became man, a concrete man, in space and time and rooted in a specific culture: 'Christ by his incarnation committed himself to the particular social and cultural circumstances of the men among whom he lived.' This is the original 'inculturation' of the word of God and is the model of all evangelization by the Church, 'called to bring the power of the Gospel into the very heart of culture and cultures' … (inculturation) means the penetration of the deepest strata of persons and peoples by the Gospel, which touches them deeply, 'going to the very center and roots' of their cultures." [58] The self emptying of God in his Son Jesus Christ who assumed a human nature in order to accomplish our salvation provides the theological paradigm for the inculturation of the Gospel in a particular human culture. The "divine pedagogy" revealed in the Incarnation is the primary theological principle for a human pedagogy through which the Gospel takes flesh in the ways of thought, values, relationships, and life of a particular culture.

The Church as culture and as agent of inculturation

A second reason for the inculturation of the Gospel is the reality and nature of the Church, the visible continuation of the life and saving mission of Christ in the world. For "the Church is both essentially human and divine, visible but endowed with invisible realities, zealous in action and dedicated to contemplation, present in the world, but as a pilgrim." [59] And while the Church exists in every culture as a "complex reality which comes together from a human and divine element," it is also true that the Church's reality and inner life *is* itself a culture. In fact, it could be argued that the success of attempts to inculturate the Gospel depends largely on the extent to which the faith of the Church is itself embodied and encountered as an organic culture, a complete way of life. When discipleship to Jesus Christ is encountered and experienced as a whole way of life, a "Christian culture," as it were, then the Gospel becomes an attractive, intelligible, and lived alternative to secular culture. Promoting and inviting others into the culture of the Church is the responsibility of the entire Christian community, with the catechist serving as "an expression and efficient instrument of this task … who, with a profound religious sense, also possesses a living social conscience and is well rooted in his cultural environment." [60]

This "culture of the Church" is constituted through the full and radiant living out of the Creed, the celebration of the sacramental life, the Christian way of life as a response of love in light of the Beatitudes and the Commandments, and the Christian spiritual tradition deepened in prayer. In this sense, the Church is considered not only as an agent of inculturation that infuses and permeates culture with the values of the Gospel, but *is* herself the living embodiment of an authentic and genuine human culture transformed by grace. The assumption underlying all catechetical efforts to inculturate the Gospel is the catechist's conviction that it is only in the light of God's grace and the power of the Holy Spirit that human culture can be transformed into a truly authentic Christian culture.

Evangelization of culture: the Church's permanent mission and identity

A third reason for the inculturation of the Gospel flows from the nature and purpose of evangelization. For we see the Church active in the evangelizing mission at the very foundation of her existence, and in every age and place ever since. In the Church's two thousand year history there has never been a time when the Church has not been fully engaged in evangelization. Is the Church's evangelizing mission a matter of historical exigency? Or is there a more fundamental reason why the Church has *always* evangelized; why the Church can never be separated from her evangelizing presence in the world?

The Church's very nature, her identity, her mission, and her purpose is to evangelize. In other words, evangelization, both old and new, is not an activity that the Church focuses on for a brief period of her history to revitalize herself from time to time. Nor is evangelization a periodic attempt to "makeover" the Church's life or a routine membership drive. It cannot be reduced to the Church's response to a particular internal crisis or external challenge. The duty and task of evangelization is intrinsic to the Church, and can therefore never be separated from her innermost reality and mission. Pope Paul VI expressed this fundamental truth in his Apostolic Exhortation, *On Evangelization in the Modern World (Evangelii Nuntiandi)*. Here is how Pope Paul VI explained the inner unity that exists between the Church and evangelization:

> Evangelizing all people constitutes the essential mission of the Church. This task and mission are particularly urgent because of the expansive, penetrating changes in present-day society. In fact, evangelizing is the grace and vocation proper to the Church; her utmost identity. She exists in order to evangelize. [61]

To say that the Church exists in order to evangelize is a reminder that evangelization is not an option for the faithful. Inasmuch as evangelization constitutes the essential mission of the Church it is also the essential mission of every baptized Catholic. But we are reminded that to say that the Church exists in order to evangelize is only half the picture. For as Father James Wehner has noted: "If the Church exists in order to evangelize, then man exists in order to be evangelized."[62]

What does it mean to say that each human person exists in order to be evangelized? Here we encounter yet another reason for the inculturation of the Gospel. For we believe that the Church evangelizes and catechizes because the mystery of each human person cannot be understood apart from the mystery of the human person in relationship to God. To be human is to be created by and for divine love. This fundamental truth is a guiding pastoral principle for the ministry of every evangelist and catechist. Our evangelizing and catechetical activity rests on the truth that the nature and purpose of each human life is fully discerned, understood, or lived only in relationship with God. As the *Catechism of the Catholic Church* (CCC 27) teaches:

> The desire for God is written in the human heart, because man is created by God and for God; and God never ceases to draw man to himself. Only in God will he find the truth and happiness he never stops searching for …

The divine-human relationship belongs to the essential nature of each human person, just as the proclamation of the Gospel belongs to the essential nature of the Church. Evangelization unites into one reality the nature and identity of the Church and the nature and identity of the human person.

Virtues of a catechist engaged in the dialogue of faith and culture

In the Church's evangelizing mission the dialogue between faith and culture, between the Church and the human person, is grounded in the concrete cultural context that shapes and informs daily life. Evangelists, catechists, preachers, teachers, and parents, strive to bridge faith and culture through a careful reading and discernment of the "signs of the times" in light of the Gospel. A catechist also cultivates and witnesses to several important virtues that we may highlight here.

The virtue of Christian hope marks the life and attitude of a catechist, particularly in the effort to inculturate the Gospel. Hope, rooted in the life, death and resurrection of Jesus Christ, allows the catechist to overcome fear and discouragement in the face of multiple cultural forces that influence and inform the daily lives of those being catechized.

The virtue of hope strengthens a catechist to avoid two extremes in the task of inculturating the Christian faith. These extreme positions not only impede the task of inculturating the Gospel, they also result in the scandal of a deeply divided Christian community. At one extreme, there is the inclination to critique, to dismiss, and to condemn all aspects of human culture. In this mode one builds walls rather than bridges between faith and culture. A solely critical stance against contemporary culture eventually leads to isolation in well-insulated and self-satisfied communities that bear little or no influence on society at large, and on the world. Fear, rather than Christian courage and hope marks this isolating impulse.

At the other extreme, there is the tendency to accommodate the Christian life to the prevailing cultural values and ways of life. Here one is casting a tightrope rather than building a sturdy bridge between faith and culture. Such an approach to contemporary culture leads toward what Fr. Aidan Nichols, O.P., has called the Church's "own internal secularization." [63] This attitude to culture leads, on a "slippery slope," to situations where the Gospel message is barely "distinguishable from everything else on offer in the market stalls of secularized religious faith." The full content of catechesis is undermined and the Gospel is no longer encountered as counter-cultural, whenever it needs to be. Instead, faith formation is reduced to a precarious tightrope walk in which the catechist's personal opinions are jumbled with the prevailing cultural world views and values. As Archbishop Augustine Di-Noia, O.P., once observed: "No one in his or her right mind will be interested in a faith about which its exponents seem too embarrassed to communicate forthrightly. We have to be convinced that the fullness of the truth and beauty of the message about Jesus Christ is powerfully attractive when it is communicated without apologies or compromise." [64]

The virtue of fidelity also marks the catechist who strives to inculturate the Gospel. A deep faithfulness to God's revelation as transmitted through Sacred Scripture and Sacred Tradition brings with it the conviction of the truths of faith, as they are believed and lived. Fidelity is not "blind obedience" to what is "imposed from above." Rather, a catechist's fidelity to the sacred deposit of faith, as summarized in the *Catechism*, is the rich fruit of prayer, and ongoing study and reflection on God's Word and the mysteries of faith. With the virtue of fidelity a catechist thinks, feels, and lives in the heart, mind, and life of the Church in a way that draws others into the living "culture of the Church."

The virtue of humility is also an essential mark of a catechist who seeks to inculturate the Gospel. In humility, a catechist is well aware of his or her own limitations in discerning and countering prevailing cultural challenges to faith formation. The catechist is always humble in the face of the task of inviting others to conversion to the Gospel way of life, always remembering that conversion is the work of the Holy Spirit, the "principal agent of evangelization." A catechist learns to rely on the interior prompting and prayerful inspiration of the Holy Spirit in witnessing to the Christian way of life as the authentic path of every human life. Attempts to inculturate the Gospel grow out of the conviction that faith that is disconnected from culture easily turns into sectarian ideology or superficial spiritualities. And culture that is not permeated with religious faith slowly, but surely, leads to the alienation and despair in individuals, the breakdown of moral norms, the fragmentation of society, and the world.

Finally there is the virtue of Christian joy that marks the witness and life of every catechist. In seeking to translate the Gospel into the language, symbols, and values of a given culture, catechists radiate a sense of enthusiasm and joy in the beauty of faith, which often convinces without the need for words. For "the world of our time, which is searching, sometimes with anguish, sometimes with hope, (needs to) receive the Good News not from evangelizers who are dejected, discouraged, impatient, or anxious, but from ministers of the Gospel whose lives glow with fervor, who have first received the joy of Christ, and who are willing to risk their lives so that the Kingdom may be proclaimed and the Church established in the midst of the world." [65]

The particular challenge facing catechists, as noted at the beginning of this chapter, is the need to present an "*inculturated catechesis.*" A catechist hopefully, faithfully, humbly, and joyfully promotes and invites others into the "culture of the Church" through the heart of human culture transformed by grace. Pastoral approaches for such an "*inculturated catechesis,*" will be the focus of the next reflections in this chapter.

An image for an "inculturated catechesis"

In the opening chapter of this book we began our reflections on the new evangelization with Pope Benedict XVI's image of entering a magnificent cathedral. As we consider the catechetical task and challenge of bridging faith and culture through an "*inculturated catechesis*" we continue our reflections with another image of a Gothic cathedral from the world of art.

> The Church evangelizes, the Church proclaims Christ, who is the Way, the Truth, and the Life; Christ who is the one mediator between God and man. And despite its human weakness, the Church never tires of proclaiming Christ.
>
> Blessed Pope John Paul II, *Crossing the Threshold of Hope*

Between 1892 and 1894, Claude Monet, the well known French Impressionist, completed a series of more than thirty paintings of Rouen Cathedral. A group of twenty works from the Rouen Cathedral series were displayed in an 1895 exhibition. Two paintings from that series may be viewed in the French Impressionist collection of the National Gallery of Art in Washington, DC. Other groupings from the series are found in museum collections around the world. In the genre of series paintings, the artist picks a single subject and renders that same subject differently to reflect various conditions of light, time of day, and weather. The emphasis is on the effect of light on forms. The subject remains constant even as the artist captures the changing effects of light and atmosphere on it.

In the Rouen Cathedral series, Monet selected a familiar motif in Western religious and cultural heritage — the Gothic cathedral. The subject of every one of the thirty or more canvases in the series is the same — the west façade of the impressive Gothic cathedral of Rouen, located about an hour north of Paris. But even as the subject of the paintings remains unchanging, no two canvases are alike. Color is the main distinguishing element in each painting named to evoke the particular view and weather conditions depicted. On one canvas after another we see the stone façade of Rouen Cathedral now bathed in the morning sunlight, now ablaze in the noonday heat, now retreating in twilight, now resting in the evening light. Or we see the same cathedral façade rising out of the morning mist, awash in the Spring rain, or bracing a wintry wind. Through this series the viewer is invited

Images courtesy of the National Gallery of Art.

to contemplate the ephemeral quality of light through the same, yet different, views of this splendid Gothic cathedral.

The Rouen Cathedral series by Claude Monet offers us a striking image for an *"inculturated catechesis"* that marks the new evangelization. In the Church's evangelizing and catechetical ministry the Gospel message that is proclaimed is the same, always and everywhere. For, "Jesus Christ is the same yesterday, and today, and forever" (Hebrews 13:8). The content of catechesis remains the same in each cultural context in which it is sown and is lived, just as the same Rouen cathedral façade is captured on each canvas in Monet's series.

While the heart of catechesis, the person of Jesus Christ, remains the same in every cultural context, each culture, with its possibilities and challenges, is like the varying conditions of light and atmosphere captured in the impressionist series. Like the varying play of light and temperature on each canvas, each culture absorbs, reflects, and lives the same Gospel message in distinct and unique ways. No two cultures receive and live the Gospel message in the exact same way. Instead, each culture, with its ways of life, its potential and limits, incarnates faith in Jesus Christ through its own particular cultural modes and manners of expression. The *General Directory for Catechesis* points to the necessity and challenge of an *"**inculturated catechesis***," when it notes:

Inculturation … is concerned to "translate" the essentials of the Gospel message into a definite cultural language. There is always tension in this necessary task: "evangelization will lose much of its power and efficacy if it does not take into consideration the people to whom it is addressed. However, it may lose its very nature and savor if on the pretext of transposing its content into another language that content is rendered meaningless or is corrupted.[66]

The task of discerning elements of American culture that resonate with or undermine the Gospel, and affirming or purifying those cultural elements in light of the Gospel, remains a key task for catechists of the new evangelization. Prayerful reflection on the ways in which culture shapes the person being catechized is a key moment in a catechist's preparation for each catechetical session. A catechist also attends to the specific ways in which the content of faith, as summarized in the *Catechism*, is either affirmed or challenged by prevailing cultural values and ways of life. Let us consider some concrete and general examples of cultural challenges that a catechist faces in each catechetical moment.

The challenge of bridging faith and culture

In turning our attention to the relationship between the Gospel and culture we are well aware that contemporary American culture presents both seemingly endless possibilities and insurmountable obstacles to the inculturation of the Gospel. While there is much to be grateful for in the life, contributions, and vitality of the Catholic Church in American culture, evangelists and catechists are also familiar with the difficulties posed by culture to ongoing faith formation. Children, young adults, and adults in faith formation programs are shaped, both consciously and unconsciously, by deep seated cultural attitudes and values, such as secularism, relativism, consumerism, materialism, and a general indifference and hostility to religion. In addressing the opening session of the Pontifical Council for the New Evangelization, Pope Benedict XVI highlighted key elements in contemporary cultural challenges to faith with these words:

> The ecumenical councils that followed sprang from the need to express the truth of revealed faith in meaningful and convincing language to people … all of this belongs to the history of evangelization, a history that developed in the encounter of the Gospel with the culture of each epoch.
>
> Blessed Pope John Paul II,
> *Crossing the Threshold of Hope*

The current crisis brings with it traces of the exclusion of God from people's lives, from a generalized indifference towards Christian faith to an attempt to marginalize it from public life … we are witnessing a drama of fragmentation which no longer admits a unifying reference point; moreover, it often occurs that people desire to belong to the Church, but they are strongly shaped by a vision of life which is in contrast to faith.[67]

The signs and symptoms of this general crisis in Catholic faith are well documented in survey after survey.[68] Church attendance in general and Mass attendance in particular has steadily declined in what has been referred to as a "quiet attrition" over several decades. Young people often fall away from active practice of the Catholic faith not long after they complete sacramental initiation. The Sacrament of Confirmation, in particular, has become for many Catholic youth the "sacrament of exit" from the Church, as observed by liturgical scholar, Aidan Kavanaugh. This gradual drifting away from active faith takes place precisely at the moment when sacramental preparation should have led a young person to full and active participation in the liturgical life of the Church and commitment to ongoing conversion and lifelong discipleship. Many young Catholics choose co-habitation in informal or open-ended living arrangements rather than preparing for and entering into the sacramental bond of marriage.

Yet another concrete outcome of the impact of cultural forces on faith formation is also confirmed repeatedly in surveys. It is the pastoral reality of Catholics whose faith formation is weak or generally wanting in content and depth. Knowledge and understanding of the basic tenets of the Catholic faith is, at best, piecemeal and, at worst, weak among significant numbers of Catholics across generations. Consequently, Catholics find themselves ill equipped to respond adequately when called to "give reasons for their hope," (1 Peter 3:15) regarding fundamental teachings of faith as summarized in the Creed, celebrated in the Sacraments, lived in the Christian moral life and deepened through prayer. This pastoral reality is routinely exploited by the secular media when covering Church issues, as seen in striking examples of public debates on the various attempts of the State to undermine the constitutional right of religious freedom of Churches and peoples of faith.

Evangelists and catechists may assume, as a pastoral given, that a significant percentage of those being formed in sacramental preparation and adult faith formation programs most likely share the negative perceptions of Catholicism held by non-Catholics and non-believers alike. These negative attitudes and misperceptions about the Catholic faith are particularly evident and widespread in the understanding and acceptance of Catholic moral precepts and teachings on family, human sexuality, and the dignity of life itself. The demoralizing effects of the clergy abuse scandals in this country and worldwide combined with growing hostility to the legitimate place of religion in the public square create an overall weakening of the influence of faith on persons and society. Finally, the systematic undermining of the constitutional right to religious freedom in this country poses a threat to every religious tradition, including the Catholic faith. While these cultural challenges are specific to this culture, they are echoed and reflected in the cultural landscape of many other societies where Christianity has ancient and historic roots. This world-wide cultural challenge to the Gospel message has been thus highlighted:

> Against the spirit of the world, the Church takes up anew each day a struggle that is none other than *the struggle for the world's soul.* If in fact, on the one hand, the Gospel and evangelization are present in this

world, on the other hand, there is also present *a powerful anti-evangelization* which is well organized and has the means to vigorously oppose the Gospel and evangelization. The struggle for the soul of the contemporary world is at its height where the spirit of this world seems strongest. [69]

Toward an "inculturated catechesis" in the new evangelization

With these theological principles that underlie genuine inculturation in mind, we turn now to consider key aspects of contemporary American culture that a catechist takes into consideration while re-proposing the Gospel today. The focus is not to provide an in-depth cultural analysis so much as to help catechists to identify, discern, and respond to the language, symbols, and dominant values of American culture that shape, influence, and inform those in our catechetical programs and religious education classrooms.

During Pope Benedict XVI's Apostolic Visit to the United States in April 2008, the Holy Father delivered a homily at a gathering of American bishops during Vespers in the Crypt Church of the Basilica Shrine of the Immaculate Conception in Washington, DC. [70] That homily remains particularly significant as the Holy Father highlighted various dimensions of contemporary American culture that are to be affirmed and purified in light of the Gospel.

Pope Benedict XVI affirmed several positive attributes of American culture, such as, the strong religious fervor among Catholics in the United States, their pride in belonging to a worshipping community, the respect for religious freedom that is deeply ingrained in the American consciousness, the generosity of those who dedicate themselves to educational and charitable activity in the name of the Church, and the rich cultural diversity of Catholics who place their traditions and gifts at the service of the Church and of society.

At the same time, the Holy Father highlighted several cultural challenges posed by contemporary American culture: secularism, materialism, and individualism. Bishops, priests, religious, and laity were encouraged to reflect systematically on the concrete ways in which the Gospel way of life resonates with the highest aspirations and achievements of contemporary American culture, as well as the multiple and deep ways in which the Christian way of life runs counter to the core values, attitudes, ways of life and message of contemporary American culture.

As catechists take up the challenge of an "*inculturated catechesis*," it is helpful to consider some of the dominant cultural aspects of American culture that shape and inform the lives of those being evangelized and catechized. Among the numerous dimensions of contemporary American culture we will focus our reflections on the following: escapism and the dominance of the media culture, secularization, individualism, and relativism. Once again, we will not attempt here a comprehensive cultural analysis of all aspects of the contemporary American cultural landscape.

The reader will find elsewhere numerous and excellent books, journals, articles, and resources dedicated to such current and contemporary cultural analysis. Rather, our aim here is simple: to invite those involved in every kind and level of faith formation to consider key aspects in the challenge of building bridges between faith and culture. The hope is that those being catechized and evangelized are continually invited into the culture of the Church, that inculturates the Gospel way of life, through the heart of American culture transformed by the light of Christian faith.

1. The catechetical challenge of a media culture of distraction and escapism

Almost anyone who participates in catechetical or faith formation programs today is directly or indirectly shaped by the common experience of the fast-paced media, entertainment, and digital culture of contemporary American society. Those we catechize may turn off their cell phones as they walk into the catechetical session, forgo their favorite television program for an evening or Sunday morning adult faith formation program, or leave behind their video games or laptop computers when they enter the classroom. But they bring with them into each catechetical moment the attitudes, values, and messages conveyed through television, the Internet, and digital and social media.

Children and teenagers in sacramental preparation programs are immersed in the phenomenon of video games, instant messaging, and social networking. It is estimated that a typical American adult may spend an average of twenty or so hours each week in front of a television screen, not to mention time spent before mobile phone and personal computer screens. Parents and educators are concerned about sensory overload on the young, and we have begun to speak of "sensory addictions" in children, young adults and adults. "Media ecology," a term introduced by educator and cultural critic, Neil Postman, is the study of communication technologies as cultural environments and the control of technology, media and communication processes on all walks of life, human perception, and relationships. The assumption is that media technologies not only serve as instruments of communication; they, in fact, create cultural environments with their own patterns of thought, behavior and life. Few will argue that through our immersion in the media saturated culture of television, the Internet, and social and digital media we may be, as it were "amusing ourselves to death" (the title of Postman's 1985 bestseller).

Those we catechize are undoubtedly formed and shaped by the values and lifestyles promoted through popular entertainment and social media. On a more fundamental level, however, they are also conditioned by the limitations and possibilities inherent in modes of communication that technology and media rely on. The very form of communications and media technology imposes limits on the content and processing of what is conveyed through them. With ever-new-and-improved information and marketing technologies, the way we experience the world changes dramatically. At best, we now have instantaneous access to large amounts of news, opinion, and information about the world, together with sophisticated and efficient means of communication that were unthinkable in previous times. At worst, the innate human capacity for sustained reflection, reasoned discourse, receptivity, interior silence and the docility of contemplation is slowly, but surely, eroding through immersion in a hurried, mouse-click paced information and media culture. In the collective attempt to keep pace with the incessant traffic of information, images, and sounds, the ability to listen attentively, to see meditatively, and to read prayerfully diminishes. *Doing*, rather than *being*, becomes the dominant mode of existence as the primary way of engaging the world is through rapidly changing information and media cycles. As our physical senses, through which we experience the world of media and digital technology, overload us with multiple images and relentless sounds, our "spiritual senses" through which we experience God are increasingly deprived of exercise, nourishment, and light.

The messages and values of the dominant entertainment culture pose yet another hurdle to faith formation as the desire for the acquisition and consumption of material goods is presented as the highest good of human existence. Carefully researched and manipulated commercial images create envy and greed, and reduce human happiness to a matter of gaining and consuming material wealth. A culture that encourages excessive materialism and wasteful consumerism reduces the human person to the sum total of their material possessions. Consequently, people are alienated from their innate human desire for transcendence and a deep hope in the life that is to come.

How then is a catechist to engage a member of the YouTube generation? How to propose friendship with and discipleship to Jesus Christ to a young person whose primary experience of friendship occurs through the technological medium of Facebook? How is a Catholic school teacher to lift the gaze of students in Christian hope toward heaven, to that which is eternal, and beyond earthly preoccupation with the acquisition and consumption of transitory material goods? How is a religious education teacher to engage in sustained reflection on the content of faith with students accustomed to "Googling" instant pieces of information in a way that excludes reflection on whether its meaningfulness can be located in a coherent and larger whole? These are only a few instances of the cultural forces that extend through mass media. In the face of the impact of such cultural forces on those being catechized, a catechist may be overwhelmed and discouraged in the catechetical task.

Catechesis in the new evangelization takes seriously the challenges posed by a dominant media culture. As part of formation it is helpful for catechists to consider both the positive and negative impact of this pervasive aspect of American culture. The benefits and inherent risks of a fast paced technology and the media culture have been described succinctly in this way:

> Today, no place in the world is beyond reach, and consequently, unaffected by the media and digital culture, which is fast becoming the "forum" of public life and social interaction. Undoubtedly, the diffusion of this culture has its benefits, including major access to information;

greater opportunities for knowledge, exchange and new forms of solidarity; and the capacity to build an increasingly "world culture" ... these potentialities, however, cannot hide the inherent risks when this kind of culture is taken to an extreme, including a selfish concentration on oneself and personal needs: an overemphasis on the emotive aspects of relations and social bonds; the loss of the objective values of experience, reflection and thought, which are reduced in many cases, to ways of reconfirming one's individualist feelings; the progressive alienation of the moral and social dimensions of life which makes others a mirror for self or simply a spectator to one's actions; and finally, the formation of a culture centered on passing novelties, the present moment and outward appearances, indeed a society which is incapable of remembering the past and with no sense of the future.[71]

To begin with, a catechist recognizes that new media is vital to proposing the Gospel anew today. A catechist will draw on some of the advantages of the media and technology culture to support faith formation. When the use of media and technology serves the content of faith then it will be beneficial to both catechist and the one being catechized. The use of digital media and communications technology is also valuable to the extent that it draws people into inter-personal relationships and into the communion of the Church, particularly at the level of the parish community. Other positive aspects of the media and digital culture that might serve the content of faith formation include rapid access to information about the Church's teachings, life and faith, greater and wider opportunities for knowledge about the teachings of the Church from reliable media sources, and the convenience of media based forums, such as blogs, for reflection and discussion on faith.

Catechists also encounter the negative effects of the sensory culture on those being catechized. Here are some pastoral approaches to assist a catechist's critical engagement with the negative influences of the media culture on those in faith formation programs:

- The prevailing media culture creates a sense of endless distraction and escapism. There is the illusory sense, conveyed through this cultural environment, that the world is a place of unending options and limitless choices, all of which are somehow "value neutral." Children, youth and adults who are addicted to the never-ending distractions offered through media and digital technologies will eventually have the innate openness to the spiritual life weakened, if not altogether blocked. In the face of this cultural challenge, a catechist will need to reawaken the God-given human capacity for prayer, silent reflection, contemplation of God's Word, and openness to mystery. Carefully planned moments at the beginning, in the middle, and at the conclusion of each catechetical session will remind those being catechized that the journey of Christian discipleship unfolds slowly in response to the inner workings of the Holy Spirit and the support of the Christian community. Catechists need to remind those in faith formation that growth in openness to and understanding the teachings of faith and living the Christian way of life require perseverance, patience, humility, and silence, all of which runs counter to the primary impulses of a fast-paced, impatient, and noisy media culture.

- To overcome the weakening of the spiritual life through immersion in media, a catechist does well to introduce those in faith formation to the ancient monastic practice of *lectio divina*. Here the emphasis is on *being* in the loving and healing presence of God, rather than escaping into the endless media driven activity of momentary distractions that marks a *doing* centered sensory culture. Pope Benedict has urged the faithful repeatedly to re-discover *lectio divina,* noting that if it is "effectively promoted, this practice will bring to the Church — I am convinced of it — a new spiritual springtime." [72] In recent years, several excellent books and resources on *lectio divina* offer insight into its history and practice. This slow, reverential, silent, and prayerful attention and reflection on the Word of God is a counter-cultural antidote to the fast paced seeing and reading culture fostered by entertainment and news technologies. In contrast to the contemporary high-speed media culture, the ancient spiritual tradition of *lectio divina* offers a distinctly Christian way of reading and hearing God's word and understanding and living the mysteries of faith. A Christian way of seeing the world with the "eyes of faith" is formed through *lectio divina,* providing an alternative to the multiple, fragmented, and often dehumanizing distractions of popular entertainment culture. Catechists may adapt the practice of *lectio divina* during a catechetical session to prepare those in faith formation to receive an important teaching of faith or to become acquainted with Christian spiritual traditions of prayer and reflection on God's word. RCIA sessions during the Lenten season could be enriched through carefully planned exercises of *lectio divina* on the Lenten Sunday Gospel readings, as spiritual preparation for the celebration of Christian initiation at Easter.

- Few will deny that there are obvious benefits to be gained from the immediate and easy access to information in a media culture. But the technologically powered availability of ready-made and instant information can result in the tendency to reduce the knowledge of faith to that which can be accessed at the speed of a computer mouse click or controlled easily. In the extreme, faith formation itself can be reduced to a matter of the individual's ability and capacity to gather pieces of information about the Catholic faith through digital and technological means. Clearly, the impersonal and isolated setting of gaining information about the faith through a Web search, for instance, runs counter to the inter-personal catechetical context in which faith is deepened and supported and the building of Christian community takes place. To engage those who may be influenced by this cultural tendency, a catechist highlights the knowledge of faith, presented in catechetical instruction, as a response to a personal God who is revealed through the Person of his Son Jesus Christ. Ultimately, a catechist invites openness and gratitude, and encourages docility to the mystery of divine revelation, received in faith as the loving and personal self-communication of God, and not simply as a body of information to be hurriedly accessed through the latest cutting edge information technologies.

- To respond to the fragmentation of knowledge into easily accessed pieces of information, a catechist will help his or her students distinguish between information that comes from knowledge and the wisdom that comes from God in the power of the Holy Spirit. In the new evangelization a catechist also emphasizes the teaching of the *Catechism* on the "analogy of faith," (CCC 114). The "analogy of faith," speaks of the inner relatedness of all the mysteries of faith — what we believe (the Creed) is lived out in the Christian moral life, and how we celebrate the Paschal Mystery of Jesus' life, death and resurrection (in the Sacraments) is deepened and nourished through the traditions of Christian prayer. All of the teachings of the *Catechism* stand in relationship to each other in a unified and organic whole centered around the person of Jesus Christ. While communications technologies give instant and ready access to immense amounts of information, it is with the "eyes of faith" that one can locate the truths of faith within the whole plan of God's saving actions in human history. The perspective of faith allows one to place isolated bits of information, gained through technology, within a larger and meaningful totality that appeals to the whole human person — mind, heart, body, spirit and soul.

- Even as "media ecology" studies technological communication as a cultural environment, the catechist extends to those in faith formation what the Church proposes as "an ecology of the human person," or "human ecology."[73] At appropriate moments a catechist encourages awareness and reflection on a "human ecology," that affirms the primacy of the human person and personal relationships in the Christian community over man-made technologies, no matter how cutting edge, convenient or efficient these may be. Catechesis on creation, "is of major importance," (CCC 279–324), to lift those submerged in the dehumanizing effects of the technological culture into of the clear light of their dignity and value as human persons, made in the image and likeness of a personal God, for union with God.

2. The challenge of secularization

The pervasive secularization that characterizes American culture today has been described and carefully analyzed by many within and outside the Catholic Church. Secularization, it has been observed, is the most potent threat to Christian faith in many of the countries of the Western world with deep Christian historical and cultural roots. There is little doubt today that secularization impacts those being formed in faith in multiple ways, both subtle and not so subtle. Therefore, an *inculturated* catechesis that serves the new evangelization takes seriously the challenge of secularization.

Pope Benedict XVI has spoken of the pervasive influence of secularization in this way:

> Secularization, which presents itself in culture by imposing a world and humanity without reference to Transcendence, is invading every aspect of daily life and developing a mentality in which God is effectively absent, wholly or partially, from human life and awareness. This secularization is not only an external threat to believers, but has been manifest for some time in the heart of the Church herself. It profoundly distorts the Christian faith from within, and consequently, the lifestyle and daily behavior of believers. They live in the world and are often marked, if not conditioned, by the cultural imagery that impresses contradictory and impelling models regarding the practical denial of God: there is no longer any need for God, to think of him or to return to him.[74]

Broadly understood, secularization is a cultural reality marked by a two-fold movement against Christian faith. On the one hand, the impulse of a secularized culture is to push Christian faith, values, attitudes, and ways of life outward to the margins of society, political, social and public life. In this way, the rightful place of religious faith, derived from the inherent religious nature of the human person, in the public square is minimized, undermined, or rendered irrelevant. On the other hand, a secularized culture pushes religious faith inward to the private sphere of human life. Secularists seek to relegate religious faith to the private realm of religious devotion and popular piety. The place and validity of public expressions of religious traditions are challenged and denied in the name of an all-encompassing "pluralism," and so-called "tolerance."

Friends, again I ask you, what about today? What are you seeking? What is God whispering to you? The hope which never disappoints is Jesus Christ. The saints show us the selfless love of his way. As disciples of Christ, their extraordinary journeys unfolded within the community of hope, which is the Church. It is from within the Church that you too will find the courage and support to walk the way of the Lord. Nourished by personal prayer, prompted in silence, shaped by the Church's liturgy you will discover the particular vocation God has for you. Embrace it with joy. You are Christ's disciples today. Shine his light upon this great city and beyond. Show the world the reason for the hope that resonates within you. Tell others about the truth that sets you free.

Pope Benedict XVI, Greeting to Young People, Saint Joseph's Seminary, New York, April 19, 2008

The origin of the word *secular* is to be found in the Latin *saecularis,* and *saeculum,* which refers to the present generation, age, century, and world. "It also connotes a culture that is purged of transcendence and reference to God in general, and the divine-human relationship that is intrinsic to the human person in particular." The forces of secularization strive to build a society devoid of any particularly religious frame of reference. In his book entitled *Secularization: Sacred Values in a Godless World,* the author Edward Norman observes, "Expressed in its greatest simplicity, (secularization) means that daily life is largely bereft of reference to religion."[75]   From a Christian perspective, the pervasiveness and deep influence of secularization directly undermine and threaten the Gospel way of life.

What is interesting for a catechist to consider is that while Christians may view secularization as an all-encompassing and potent threat to faith and the Christian life, many people, even those in our catechetical and faith formation programs may not view as problematic its influence and growth. Even as they absorb, knowingly or unknowingly, the values, attitudes, lifestyles, and worldviews of a secularized culture, many people equate secularization with all that is true and fulfilling of human potential and the advancement of society. Such misperceptions about the outcome of secularization are a unique challenge for those responsible for faith formation. Here is how this particular aspect of secularization has been described:

> Many view the secularizing trend, in a positive sense, as a liberation from the things of the past or as the way completely to separate any idea of the transcendent from the world and humanity. Although anti-Christian, anti-religious and anti-clerical references are sometimes heard today, secularism, in recent times, has not taken the form of a direct, outright denial of God, religion or Christianity. Instead, the secularizing movement has taken a more subtle tone in cultural forms which invade people's everyday lives and foster a mentality in which God is completely or partially left out of life and human consciousness. In this way, secularism has entered the Christian life and ecclesial communities and has become not simply an external threat for believers but something to be faced each day in life in the various manifestations of the so-called culture of relativism.[76]

Catechists have before them a two-fold task in countering the effects of secularization: to respond to the practical effects of secularization and to counter the pervasive notion that secularization is somehow beneficial to society or that a secularized culture promotes genuine human freedom and happiness. Here we may consider some pastoral emphases in a catechist's critical engagement with the negative forces of secularization on those in faith formation programs:

- Catechesis on the nature of Christian faith (CCC 142–197) helps those immersed in a secularizing culture to understand the rightful and vital place of faith in society. Faith is a free, human response to God's revelation. As a human act, faith originates in the religious nature of the human person. As

Pope Benedict XVI notes: "There is a deep hunger that only God can satisfy. Human beings of the third millennium want an authentic, full life; they need truth, profound freedom, love freely given. Even in the deserts of the secularized world, man's soul thirsts for God, for the living God. [77] We believe that "the desire for God is written on each human heart," and that to be human is to search for and to live in relationship with God. Therefore, faith cannot be reduced to a matter of private superstition or relegated to the margins of society and public discourse. Catechists lead those catechized to understand that secularization not only denies the contribution of the Church and religious faith to the public sphere; secularization essentially amounts to a denial of the human person in their totality, in *his* or *her* own totality. A secularized culture represents not only an assault on the Church and people of religious faith, but is, at heart, an undermining of the dignity and nature of the human person, who is an essentially religious being. As Blessed Pope John Paul II noted on his first Apostolic Visit to Poland: "The exclusion of Christ from the history of man is an act against man" (Blessed Pope John Paul II, Homily at Victory Square, Warsaw, June 2, 1979).

- Catechesis on the Fall and the reality of human sinfulness (CCC 385–421) helps to counter the subtle and not so subtle influences of the secularization of culture. The secularist's creed is that the human person is invincible and beyond reproach. Human weakness and the degradations of humanity are explained away or reduced to social, psychological, and biological forces. The fundamental spiritual root of our fallen human condition is overlooked in favor of psychological, social, genetic, scientific, and even technological reductions of the human person. In the face of this secularizing tendency, catechists do well to teach, clearly and with charity, on the reality of human sinfulness, as evidenced at every level of human relationships — personal, communal, and global. For without a sense of the radical weakness of the human condition and the reality of human sinfulness, it makes no sense to speak of the need for redemption from sin and the need for salvation that comes from God. As Edward Norman concludes:

> The religion which Christ came to deliver is about the inability of men and women to put what is wrong with themselves right. It is about human sin, and the flawed nature of each person which renders everyone incapable of self-redemption. Here, as it happens, encased within its very starkness, is the spiritual beauty of Christianity — and the reason why it will endure till the end of time. For Christianity is centered in the phenomenon which is outside of human control … the Christian hope is precisely derived from the fact that God loves us in spite of what we are. The religion of Jesus will endure because, alone among the religious systems of the world, and elevated not by

human estimation and numerical support (but by the man who was God and who died because of our sins) it is a religion which is realistically addressed to our fallen nature. Jesus called people to repentance; that was his priority and it ought to be the priority of the modern Church. And indeed, it *is* the priority of … those who truly are the body of Christ in the world, loyal to his teaching, wretched in the horrific facts of their humanity, but made spiritually serene by the great love of God. [78]

- Catechists will encourage those being catechized to recover a confident, joyful and charitable courage in witnessing to their Catholic faith in the public sphere. This public witness to faith that each priest, religious, and lay Catholic gives is the concrete means by which the heart of human culture is transformed by the light of the Gospel. A catechist calls to mind the distinct role and duty of the laity to "consecrate the world to God" through the daily living out of the Gospel. This "lived evangelization" takes place in and through Christian witness to the sanctity of marriage and consecrated life, in family life, neighborhoods, and in the political and social spheres. Finally, catechists engage in an inculturated catechesis that responds to the dynamic of secularization by helping the laity to recover their rightful role and vocation, described in the teachings of the Second Vatican Council:

> In the Church there is a diversity of ministry but unity of mission … the laity, have therefore, in the Church and in the world, their own assignment in the mission of the whole People of God. In the concrete their apostolate is exercised when they work at the evangelization and sanctification of men; it is exercised too when they endeavor to have the Gospel permeate and improve the temporal order, going about it in a way that bears clear witness to Christ and helps forward the salvation of all people. The characteristic of the lay state being a life lived in the midst of the world and of secular affairs, the laity are called by God to make of their apostolate, through the vigor of their Christian spirit, a leaven in the world. [79]

3. The challenge of individualism

Yet another contemporary cultural challenge for evangelization, catechesis, and faith formation is the deep seated individualism that marks American culture. Images of the "rugged individual" asserting the cherished ideal of self determination are so ingrained in American consciousness making it all the more difficult to recognize individualism as a cultural problem that needs to be purified in light of the Gospel. "Temptations to superficiality and self-centeredness, arising from a predominating hedonistic and consumer-oriented mentality, are not easily overcome. The 'death of God' announced decades ago by so many intellectuals has given way to an unproductive cult of the individual." [80]

This cultural challenge finds visual expression in entertainment, advertizing, commercials, and mass media. It is the promotion of a "cult of the individual," in which individual freedom, autonomy and rejection of authority, and the illusion of self-dependency are exalted at the expense of personal responsibility, accountability to community and society, and mutual interdependence. More importantly, the "cult of individualism" promotes the view that faith is anti-individual and that to be a person of faith is to be less free, less human, less of an individual.

- To engage the cultural challenge of individualism catechesis affirms the dignity of each human person in the light of Christ (CCC 1730–1748). Once again, a sound catechesis on creation is invaluable in helping to counter the effects of an individualistic culture. We are created as persons in community, not as isolated individuals. As human persons we are created for union through love of God and neighbor, not for isolation that leads to despair. The reduction of the human person to an isolated self-referencing individual harms, not advances, the dignity of each human life that originates in God's creative love. A catechist may evoke or draw on common human experiences of personal isolation, fragmentation, and confusion that marks an individualistic culture and offer the invitation to full belonging and participation in the Church experienced as the People of God, the Body of Christ, and the Temple of the Holy Spirit.

- The Gospel of Jesus Christ does not devalue or constrain individual freedom; it simply locates that freedom within the demands of love of God and neighbor. Through faith formation a person comes to recognize freedom as a gift from God and as a responsibility to others, not as open-ended license or as self-preservation. Through catechesis on the Christian moral life a person is led to understand and to exercise freedom as a response to God's law of love. In this way, "freedom attains perfection in its acts when directed toward God, the sovereign Good" (CCC 1744).

This counter-cultural element of catechesis is important particularly for faith formation with youth and young children. Formed by the values of an individualistic culture, young people in catechetical formation programs are shaped by the "cult of the individual," individual autonomy and the rejection of authority, including the authority of the Church. A full catechesis on freedom (CCC 1730–1748) leads children, young adults, and adults to see that the exercise of individual human freedom with little or no reference to the demands of divine and human love serves only the self-centered and competing rights of isolated individuals, ultimately leading to the fragmentation of families, communities and society itself.

- A catechist looks for catechetical opportunities to counter the cultural assumption that the Church and faith in Jesus Christ is somehow anti-human or anti-individual. Catechesis on the nature of the Church (CCC 748–810) reaffirms that Christ and the Church walk the path of every human person.

Catechesis on the nature of man created in the image and likeness of God affirms the goodness of the human person as the *Catechism* teaches, "Being in the image of God the human individual possesses the dignity of a person, who is not just something, but someone. He is capable of self-knowledge, of self-possession and of freely giving himself and entering into communion with other persons. And he is called by grace to a covenant with his Creator, to offer him a response of faith and love that no other creature can give in his stead" (CCC 357).

"Man is the way of the Church," as Blessed Pope John Paul II repeatedly affirmed. Catechesis draws on a fundamental teaching of the Second Vatican Council that affirms that, "In reality it is only in the mystery of the Word made flesh that the mystery of man truly becomes clear … Christ fully reveals man to man himself and makes his supreme calling clear" (*Gaudium et Spes*, 22).

- Through catechesis on the Sacraments, particularly the Eucharist (CCC 1322–1419), a catechist leads others to overcome the influence of individualism. The Sacraments make possible our union with Christ and with one another in the community of the Church. In the sacrament of the Eucharist, "we unite ourselves to Christ, who makes us sharers in His Body and Blood to form a single body" (CCC 1331). In the mystery of the Eucharist we find the concrete response of faith to the cultural challenge to faith posed by individualism.

- Finally, an inculturated catechesis responds to the misperception that faith in Jesus Christ implies a denial or diminishing of individual fulfillment and happiness. Catechesis on Christian discipleship offers a concrete alternative to individualism as it leads the disciple of Christ to the genuine gift of self as the path to authentic human happiness and personal fulfillment. Catechesis also affirms that:

  > In the Christian understanding, authentic interpersonal communion presupposes the full realization, not the absorption or suppression of the individual persons who enter into it. Thus, if Christ, is to be the pattern for the transformation accomplished in us by the Holy Spirit, it can only mean that in being conformed to him, we each discover and realize our unique identities as persons. This is an immense and astonishing claim…. "For whoever wants to save his life will lose it, and whoever loses his life for my sake will find it" (Matt 16:25)…. Here Christ asserts, in effect, that each person will find his or her true self only by being conformed to Christ … only the Son of God could make such a claim on us. Only the perfect image of God who is the person of the Son could constitute the principle

and pattern for the transformation and fulfillment of every human person who has ever lived. The more we are conformed to his image, the more authentically we become our true selves.[81]

4. The challenge of relativism

In a homily given during the Mass for the Election of the Roman Pontiff on the eve of his election to the papacy, Pope Benedict XVI spoke of what he termed a "dictatorship of relativism." He noted that "we are building a dictatorship of relativism that does not recognize anything as definitive and whose ultimate goal consists solely of one's own ego and desires." [82] Of particular interest to catechists is the impact of the cultural reality of relativism on the offer, acceptance, and lived expression of faith. The Holy Father noted that it has become commonplace that those who live according to "a clear faith based on the Creed of the Church" are considered extreme. At the same time, a deep seated relativism that allows "letting oneself be 'tossed here and there, carried out by every wind of doctrine,' is exalted as good for the individual and for society." A few years earlier, then-Cardinal Joseph Ratzinger observed that relativism may, in fact, be "the greatest problem of our time." [83]

> Man in the full truth of his existence … in the sphere of his own family, in the sphere of society … in the sphere of his own nation or people … and in the sphere of the whole of mankind … this man is the primary route that the Church must travel in fulfilling her mission.
>
> Blessed Pope John Paul II,
> *Redeemer of Man*, 10

Broadly speaking, relativism is the notion that truth is only relative to that which each person or culture or society holds. There are no universal and absolute truths. Instead, relativism holds that truth changes from one person to another and from one historical and cultural context to another. A relativist denies that objective truth exists. And if some form of objective truth does exist, a relativist denies the God-given human capacity for objectively revealed and held truths. Those who espouse these views can be seen as moral relativists and as religious relativists.

For a relativist the only truth that is objective is that which can be scientifically measured and verified. Everything about human existence and relationships is a matter of subjective opinion, based on individual tastes, culture and history. In a relativistic society the highest moral norm is "tolerance" of all opinions and values that are considered equal. Whether or not a moral action or societal value conforms to the dignity of the human person or the revelation that comes from God is considered irrelevant. In a relativistic world there are no objectively received and held truths about God or objective moral truths about how we are to live and act in relationship to one another. A relativist allows only for a multitude of opinions that are equally valid in their claims to be true or to carry moral weight. As one author puts it, "relativists hold that there are no right and wrong moral choices; rather, right and wrong are *relative* to one's feelings, sentiments, or cultural milieu. But one look at moral atrocity shows us that this cannot be true … some choices are clearly right and others are clearly wrong … because it is impossible for relativism to be consistent, many people end up being 'selective relativists,' objective about things they feel strongly about (terrorism? gun control? global warming?) but nothing else (sexual ethics? religion?)." [84]

Once the question of objective truth is bracketed out a person is left only with questions that deal with practical usefulness and material gain. A person who accepts and lives by a relativistic worldview is enclosed within a system of ideological power, utilitarian pleasure or materialistic gain. As then Cardinal Ratzinger noted in a reflection on Blessed Pope John Paul II's encyclical *Fides et Ratio*:

> The modern attitude reveals at the same time a false humility and a false presumption: a false humility that does not recognize in the human person the capacity for the truth; a false presumption by which one places oneself above things, above truth itself, while at the same time making the extension of one's power, one's domination over things, the objective of one's thoughts ... (*Fides et Ratio)* seeks to restore to humanity the courage to seek the truth, that is, to encourage reason once again in the adventure of search for truth ... man is not trapped in a hall of mirrors of interpretations; one can and must seek a breakthrough to what is really true; man must ask who he really is and what he is to do; he must ask whether there is a God, who God is and what the world is. The one who no longer poses these questions is by that very fact bereft of any standard or path. [85]

Let us consider for a moment how a relativistic worldview impacts the minds and hearts of children, youth, and adults in faith formation programs. First, we recognize that while many of those in faith formation programs hold to a relativistic worldview they may not be aware of it or may never have even given it a name! They simply hold this view of life and have never reflected on how it runs deeply counter to a genuine life of faith in God within the life of the Church. They also may never have considered that holding to absolute relativism is a contradiction in terms. To say with absolute certainty that there is no objective truth is to propose that one claim as objective truth. The relativists' claim itself presupposes that objective truth does exist! Here is how one author describes well the inherent flaw of relativism:

> The one "dogma" of relativism is that it is absolutely true for everyone that nothing is absolutely true for everyone. This claim can't be true because it contradicts itself — it's what we call a self-contradictory proposition. If it's true for everyone that nothing is true for everyone, then the statement, "Nothing is true for everyone" also isn't true for everyone! [86]

There are several ways in which relativism impacts the Church's ministry of catechesis that unfolds in catechetical settings and classrooms. For one, when the truths of faith are presented with certainty they are met with an implicit skepticism. This ingrained attitude of doubt or a "hermeneutic of suspicion" has roots in a relativistic mindset. From this perspective anyone or any religious tradition that proposes objective truths of faith is implicitly considered "rigid," "narrow-minded," and even "intolerant." The challenge is for catechists to lead those in faith formation out of the self-contradictory enclosure of relativism into the clear light and fresh air of objective truths revealed by God that alone give ultimate meaning and purpose to life. As the *Doctrinal Note on Some Aspects of Evangelization* highlights:

> Today, with ever increasing frequency, questions are being raised about the legitimacy of presenting to others — so that they might in turn accept it — that which is held to be true for oneself. Often this is seen as an infringement of other people's freedom. Such a vision of human freedom, separated from its integral reference to truth is one of the expressions "of that relativism which, recognizing nothing as definitive, leaves as the ultimate criterion only the self with its desires and under the semblance of freedom, becomes a prison for each one" … a legitimate plurality of positions has yielded to an undifferentiated pluralism, based upon the assumption that all positions are equally valid, which is one of today's most widespread symptoms of the lack of confidence in the truth … if man denies his fundamental capacity for the truth, if he becomes skeptical regarding his ability really to know what is true, he ends up losing what in a unique way draws his intelligence and enthralls his heart. [87]

In almost every catechetical setting a catechist will encounter various forms of a relativistic worldview expressed in claims about and objections to faith. For instance, we may hear it said that all religious traditions are equally valid and true ways of approaching God. For any one religious tradition to claim to receive divinely revealed truths from God is dismissed as intolerant. From a relativistic stance a young person may challenge a catechist by saying that while Jesus may be God for one individual, the Buddha may be God for another person and that this is simply a matter of individual preference. In the moral sphere, the Church's moral teachings on the sacredness of life and human sexuality are questioned and rejected on the premise that it is intolerant to impose a set of moral values on another. We may hear it said that what is morally good and true for one person need not be morally good and true for another. The claim of any one religious tradition to objective moral truths is deemed "narrow" and "intolerant." Finally, God is nothing more than what each individual person creates or projects out of the store of his or her own personal history, imagination, and experiences. "By subjectifying God, relativism sets us up as creators of God rather than God as the Creator of us." [88]

- To begin to engage a relativistic mindset in the catechetical setting, a catechist will teach clearly and lovingly about the nature of God as a personal Being whose existence does not depend on our human creation. Catechesis on the first article of the Creed concerning God as Creator is critical to countering a relativistic view of God. A catechist gently leads others to an understanding of the actual Being of God who exists as a personal reality beyond human reason, imagination, and experience and who, by definition, is not subject to the confines of human reason, human imagination or experience. Very often, as evidenced in many conversion stories, a person's encounter with the awesome reality and sheer gift of God's being as transcendent, mysterious, and totally other becomes a true moment of grace and the beginnings of a deep intellectual and moral conversion.

- To counter the effects of relativism in the minds and hearts of those being catechized, a catechist will need to engage in discussions about the nature and characteristics of faith itself (CCC 153–184). Christian faith is that which we do not create ourselves, but which is ultimately received as sheer grace and gratuitous gift. To reduce faith to a matter of personal preference is to simply live one's life at the whim of human opinions, and not genuine and certain truths that God has given us of Himself that alone provide ultimate meaning and purpose to life. Only that which is received from above, from God, is in fact worthy of the entrusting of one's entire life and love. To base one's whole life simply on individual preferences and human opinions that shift and change easily, and that are relative to time and place, is like building and living in a house on shifting sand. The certainty of revealed truth that comes from divine Revelation, that is the basis of Christian faith, is affirmed as the answer to the deepest desires of the human heart and mind for authentic and stable purpose and meaning in life. Human beings need certainty about matters of faith and morals because our human nature demands it and because the answers proposed through faith are ultimately matters of life and death. As Chris Stefanick notes, "The stakes are high when it comes to the meaning of life (faith) and how we should live it (morals). Such things cut to the very heart of the purpose of our existence and how we should live it out. Only a high degree of surety about these things can give us the confidence we need to face life with a firm sense of purpose and death with hope."[89]

- From time to time set aside moments in your catechetical sessions to briefly discuss the characteristics of faith, even as you present different areas of catechetical content. With a firm understanding of the nature of faith itself, the hearts and minds of your listeners will be better prepared to receive and live the content of catechesis. Remind your students that understanding and believing in religious and moral truths is possible only by God's grace and the help of the Holy Spirit. Begin and end your catechetical sessions with a prayer for the grace of the Holy Spirit who opens the heart and mind to the mysteries of faith and to the truths that come from God. Remind your students of the grace that comes with faith that opens "the eyes of (their) hearts" to understand and live the contents of Revelation as expressed in the *Catechism*. More importantly, "trusting in God and cleaving to the truths he had revealed are contrary neither to human freedom nor to human reason" (CCC 154). Just as it is not contrary to human dignity or freedom to trust in what others tell us in our various human relationships, in the same way it does not diminish our freedom or dignity to place our trust in the truths that come from God. In fact, when we do so, our dignity and freedom as children of God is affirmed in the deepest possible way.

- To counter the implicit and explicit presuppositions of a relativistic world-view, a catechist reminds those in faith formation that the Church does not impose her faith. Rather, Christian faith is proposed as the way to live a fully human life in God. By virtue of Baptism faith makes us a new creation in Christ in the power of the Holy Spirit who unites us into the community of the Church. The offer of faith is freely given and freely accepted, in keeping with the full dignity of the human person and the freedom that comes from God. Affirming the gratuitous nature of faith and the freedom of every believer counters the false relativistic notion that religious traditions somehow impose beliefs and deny human freedom.

- A catechist instills confidence in the human ability to know and to live by religious and moral truths rooted in the human faculties of intellect and will that are given by God. Since this confidence in the human capacity for truth is steadily eroded in a relativistic culture, a catechist will need to inspire, time and time again, an awareness and humble confidence in our God given desire and capacity for truth that can be known with certainty. For, "the Church, holds and teaches that God, the first principle and last end of all things, can be known with certainty from the created world by the natural light of human reason. Without this capacity, man would not be able to welcome God's revelation. Man has this capacity because he is created in the "image of God" (CCC 36).

  To counter the effects of relativism we affirm gently and defend firmly this human capacity to know God through reason and in faith. We teach about both the human capacity and the limits of reason in coming to know religious and moral truths (CCC 36–43). This is a valuable gift that a catechist gives to those in faith formation who may be influenced by relativism. Through faith formation a person comes to recognize that he or she "is by nature and vocation a religious being. Coming from God, going toward God, man lives a fully human life only if he freely lives by his bond with God" (CCC 44). Through catechetical instruction and formation, this recognition of one's innate desire and capacity for revealed truth is received as a gift of faith that fully accords with human dignity and authentic freedom.

- In a relativistic worldview the only knowledge that is considered certain is that which can be empirically measured and verified. Religious truths that cannot be verified scientifically are dismissed as an inferior form of knowing. In presenting the faith of the Church, a catechist invites those in faith formation to recognize that the knowledge that comes from faith is a form of knowledge that is certain, equally valid, and consequential for the whole of one's life. While science may provide hypothetical or definitive knowledge about the natural and material world, Christian faith proposes divinely revealed truths about spiritual and eternal realities. These forms of knowledge are not contradictory but together point to the beauty and intelligibility of the created world and the human person as the crown of God's creation. In fact, "faith is more certain than all human knowledge because it is founded on the very word of God who cannot lie … revealed truths can seem obscure to human reason and experience, but 'the certainty that the divine light gives is greater than that which the light of natural reason gives.' 'Ten thousand difficulties do not make one doubt'" (CCC 157).

- Finally, a catechist will be called to respond to the relativistic view that the Church is "intolerant" by the very fact that it makes truth claims about God, about His Son Jesus Christ, about the Church, and about the Christian way of life. This particular dimension of relativism undermines faith formation because it places a negative moral value on the core of the catechetical act as it assumes, conveys, and forms others in objective truths of faith. In responding to this particular catechetical challenge, a catechist invites those in faith formation to understand the nature of divine Revelation and the nature of the Church as One, Holy, Catholic, and Apostolic. The catechist also highlights the nature of human freedom that can never be separated from reference to truth (CCC 1730–1748). The truth claims of Christianity are never offered as an opportunity to denigrate or degrade the claims of other religious traditions. Rather they are proposed for the hearts and minds of all those who seek truth, goodness and beauty. In her truth claims about God and the divine-human relationship, the Church proposes to the world the divine Person of Jesus Christ as "the Way, the Truth, and the Life." This proposal of faith, at the heart of catechesis and evangelization, is rooted in the Church's origin and identity.

In this third chapter we have reflected on the challenges of presenting an "inculturated catechesis" that takes into consideration some of the dominant features of American culture as it shapes the hearts and minds of those in catechetical formation. We have considered possible catechetical approaches to engage positively those challenges posed by the media culture, secularism, individualism, and relativism. Your discussion and reflection on these themes will no doubt yield further insights drawn from your catechetical experience and wisdom.

In responding to the challenges posed by culture a catechist seeks to build bridges between faith and life, between the mysteries of faith and human experience. In each catechetical context, a catechist strives to inculturate the Gospel in a way that transforms both positive and negative elements of culture in the light of faith. A catechist remains joyful and hopeful in the face of the many cultural opportunities and challenges faced in catechesis that serve the new evangelization. For,

> We are facing situations which are signs of massive changes, often causing apprehension and fear. These situations require a new vision, which allows us to look to the future with eyes full of hope and not with tears of despair … we oftentimes feel unable to enflesh this vision, in other words, to "make it our own" and "to bring it to life" for ourselves and the people we meet every day, and to make it the basis for the Church's life and all her pastoral activities … a new evangelization means to share the world's deep desire for salvation and render our faith intelligible by communicating the *logos* of hope (cf. 1 Peter 3:15). Humanity needs hope to live in these present times. The content of this hope is "God who has a human face and who has 'loved us to the end'" … each person today, whether he knows it or not, needs this proclamation … this is the reason for renewing the appeal for a new evangelization, not simply as an added responsibility but as a way to restore joy and life to situations imprisoned in fear.[90]

Questions for Reflection and Discussion

1. Discuss three reasons why the inculturation of the Gospel is an essential element of catechesis in the new evangelization.

2. Share concrete challenges from those you catechize that are rooted in the cultural forces of secularism, individualism, and relativism.

3. Discuss concrete ways in which you can draw on the practical approaches offered in this chapter to respond to the influence of cultural forces on those you form in faith.

CHAPTER FOUR

Rediscovering the *Catechism of the Catholic Church* as a Vital Tool of the New Evangelization

Perhaps you have watched or heard of the television series, *The Antiques Roadshow*. It may even be a favorite of yours. On this popular public television program a crew of expert antique appraisers travel to various cities across the country. People from all walks of life bring their assorted treasures to be appraised. Some bring precious family heirlooms carefully handed down from generation to generation, others bring assorted trinkets discovered unexpectedly in yard sales or antique shops, and still others bring long forgotten curios gathering dust in attics or basements. With their keen observation and expert knowledge of antiques, the appraisers offer detailed explanations of the history and auction value of each item to its owner. Each episode in the series unfolds as the antique owner is either delighted or disappointed to learn from the expert appraiser the real worth and true value of their treasure.

The treasure of the *Catechism of the Catholic Church*

The *Catechism of the Catholic Church* is a treasure and gift of faith. But like any treasure its true value and catechetical riches may need to be rediscovered from time to time. One such opportune moment is the Year of Faith that begins on October 11, 2012. During this Year of Faith, all Catholics are encouraged to return to the depth and breadth of Church teaching contained in this treasure of faith. In particular, catechists and evangelists are invited to discover, once again, the inexhaustible riches of catechetical content contained in the *Catechism,* and to place this treasure at the service of the new evangelization.

For some, the rediscovery of the *Catechism* may involve taking up anew a catechetical tool that is used frequently and consistently in faith formation. In this case a catechist will return to a familiar and trusted catechetical resource. For others, it might mean retrieving a copy of the *Catechism* that has perhaps gathered dust on a shelf over the years. Whatever the case may be, the invitation and challenge is the same: to grow in knowledge and understanding of the content of the *Catechism* and to experience a renewed confidence in this catechetical treasure as the complete, authentic, and sure point of reference for the faith formation of children, young adults, and adults alike.

To aid catechists toward a renewed appreciation of the *Catechism* as a vital tool of the new evangelization, this chapter highlights three key points for reflection and discussion. We will consider the following three topics:

1. Why do we have or need the *Catechism*?

2. What is the *Catechism of the Catholic Church*, its origin, and purpose?

3. And what are some "best practices" to guide the use of the *Catechism* at the service of the new evangelization?

These themes may also be used to guide a "study day" on the *Catechism of the Catholic Church,* before or during the Year of Faith. The hosting of "study days" on the *Catechism* is encouraged in the *Note with Pastoral Recommendations for the Year of Faith.* Such study days are typically part of ongoing catechist formation programs. The themes offered here present one practical way for catechists to reflect on and renew their appreciation for the breadth, depth and beauty of the Catholic faith, as presented in the *Catechism*.

1. Why we have or need the *Catechism of the Catholic Church*

Imagine for a moment that you are a physics teacher offering an introductory course, say Physics 101, to high school students. On the first day of class you explain the course syllabus and set the stage for the overall content of the course. You begin by telling the students that their study of physics will not be shaped by the laws of nature or established laws and scientific theories in the field of physics. Commonly accepted theories of motion, gravity, and light, will be considered only as suggestions, not laws that guide the study of physics. The whole point is that students will generate their own scientific laws and theories as they go along. You inform your students that one of the course outcomes is that they are to arrive at their own personal understanding and conclusions about the science of physics.

There's no doubt you will get some very puzzled looks from your students at this point. Perhaps even a few raised hands from students who question how the course as you propose it can proceed effectively. Even students with minimal knowledge of the subject matter will grasp instinctively that the proposed course will be self-defeating to their study of physics. Their discomfort at the proposed physics course is rooted in a fundamental presupposition of any field of human knowledge. In any area of human inquiry we assume that knowledge proceeds by way of commonly held first principles, fundamental laws, and theoretical propositions, from which are drawn further principles and practical applications. Without some commonly held foundational principles the exercise of coming to know, learn, and understand any field of human knowledge is tenuous and absurd, if not unattainable.

Catechesis as the organic formation and systematic instruction in the content of the Catholic faith is unlike teaching the disciplines of science. For one, science is based on observation of the natural world, and the gathering of empirical evidence that is measured and verified. But like the sciences, the handing on of the content of faith also begins with first principles and foundational propositions, received and adhered to in faith. This content of faith is given to us in the *Catechism of the Catholic Church.* For the *Catechism* contains "a statement of the Church's faith and of Catholic doctrine, attested to or illumined by Sacred Scripture, the Apostolic Tradition, and the Church's Magisterium … (it is) a sure norm for teaching the faith and thus a valid and legitimate instrument for ecclesial communion." [91] In other words, the *Catechism* presents to the faithful and to the world an authentic and authoritative summary of the foundational principles of the Catholic faith, as believed, celebrated, lived and prayed.

As catechists we might ask ourselves, then: How often is the *Catechism* received as a gift and treasure that presents the fundamental principles of the Catholic faith? And is it not the case that this purpose of the *Catechism* is misunderstood, more often than not, by those we are privileged to form in faith? For this reason, it is helpful to begin this reflection by considering first why the Church presents us with a universal *Catechism.* This initial reflection prepares both catechists and those being catechized to be receptive to its teachings with gratitude and openness, and with the conviction and certainty of faith.

Receiving the *Catechism of the Catholic Church* as gift and treasure

So before we consider the origin and purpose of the universal *Catechism* or discuss some "best practices" for its use as a vital tool of the new evangelization, let us take a moment to reflect on the question, Why do we have or need the *Catechism of the Catholic Church*? This discussion engages various misconceptions and barriers to receiving and understanding the *Catechism,* and opens the way to recognize and receive the *Catechism* as a gift and treasure of faith.

Most catechists will readily acknowledge the *Catechism* as a point of reference in catechetical formation and preparation. But those we evangelize and catechize may not always recognize its value. Yet we know that a renewal of catechesis in our time depends on the extent to which both catechists and those in faith formation rediscover the *Catechism* as a vital tool in the new evangelization.

Divine Revelation — a foundational principle of faith and of catechesis that guides the use of the *Catechism of the Catholic Church*

In catechetical ministry, the content of instruction and formation of children, youth, young adults, and adults is shaped by divine Revelation. This is a fundamental starting point for all forms of catechetical ministry. The content of catechesis, derived from divine Revelation and transmitted through Sacred Scripture and Sacred Tradition, is presupposed as the foundational principle for catechetical instruction and faith formation. The whole saving plan of God's self-communication as it unfolds in human history and the human response of faith to God is understood as one of the most fundamental tenets of Christian faith and the essential content of catechesis. For,

> It is on the basis of revelation that catechesis will try to set its course, revelation as transmitted by the universal Magisterium of the Church, in its solemn or ordinary form. This revelation tells of a creating and redeeming God, whose Son has come among us in our flesh and enters not only into each individual's personal history but into human history itself, becoming its center ... if conceived in this way catechesis ... goes beyond any kind of temporal, social and political "messianism." It seeks to arrive at man's innermost being.[92]

The *Catechism* teaches that God can be known with certainty from the created world by the natural light of human reason. We stand in need of divine Revelation because of the limits and weaknesses of human reason. For "by natural reason man can know God with certainty, on the basis of his works ... (but) there is another order of knowledge, which man cannot possibly arrive at by his own powers: the order of divine Revelation. Through an utterly free decision, God has revealed himself and given himself to man ... God has fully revealed this plan by sending us his beloved Son, our Lord Jesus Christ, and the Holy Spirit" (CCC 50). While the whole plan of God's self-communication in divine Revelation is the full content of catechesis, it is the person of Jesus Christ and our relationship to him as Christian disciples that stands at the heart of catechetical formation.

The prevailing cultural values of secularism, relativism, and individualism lead many to reject, implicitly or explicitly, this foundational principle of divine Revelation, particularly as the content of faith takes the form of doctrines. This mindset has deep roots in the Enlightenment philosophies of rationalism and scientific positivism. Without going into lengthy analysis of the philosophical presuppositions of these worldviews here, it is helpful for catechists to be aware of and to recognize the pastoral and practical effects of such worldviews in those we are privileged to catechize and evangelize.

A rationalist worldview carries with it the assumption that doctrines and creeds undermine the full exercise of human reason. To accept in faith the dogmas of faith is seen as burdensome and limiting the full flourishing of individual autonomy. To hold to a set of doctrines that have been handed down as a "sacred deposit of faith" is therefore cast aside as the expression of an outmoded, antiquated pre-scientific worldview. Revealed doctrines, and established dogmas and creeds of institutional religions are implicitly and explicitly rejected in favor of a creed-less, doctrine-less spirituality whereby one picks and chooses or makes up one's beliefs as you go along. In this world view, the acceptance of doctrines and the revealed truths of faith is seen as contrary to reason and to human freedom. From an individualistic and rationalistic perspective the doctrines of revealed religion are to be shed as shackles confining the autonomous exercise of enlightened reason and human freedom.

As noted by Pope Benedict XVI, "To a greater extent than in the past, faith is now being subjected to a series of questions arising from a changed mentality that, especially today, limits the field of rational certainties to that of scientific and technological discoveries … human reason, in fact bears within itself a demand for 'what is perennially valid and lasting.' This demand constitutes a permanent summons, indelibly written into the human heart, to set out to find the One whom we would not be seeking had he not already set out to meet us. To this encounter, faith invites us." [93]

The Church's catechetical ministry rests on the assumption that the faith that we profess in the Creed has a specific content shaped by divine Revelation and transmitted in Sacred Scripture and Sacred Tradition. Christianity is a religion of the Word made flesh, the Incarnation of God in the divine person of His Son, Jesus Christ, who reveals the mysterious and saving plan of God. While the various religions of the world attest to the human search for God, Christianity alone claims that God comes in human flesh to meet man in friendship and love. Through the gradual unfolding of divine Revelation, God comes in search of humanity. God's desire to reconcile all of humanity to himself in love reaches its fullness in the sending of his own Son.

Through Jesus Christ all of creation is invited to share in the divine nature, so as to be reconciled to the Father, through Christ, the Word made flesh, in the Holy Spirit. It is God who has chosen to reveal Himself in this way — through the person of His Son, Jesus Christ in the power of the Holy Spirit. The living transmission by the Church of this divine Revelation in Sacred Scripture and Sacred Tradition guarantees that what is received in faith is not simply the best expressions of human reason or human ingenuity, but is, in fact, that by which "God has revealed himself to man by gradually communicating his own mystery in deeds and in words" (CCC 69). The priority of divine Revelation and the nature of Christian faith as the response to God's revelation is the basis for receiving the content of faith as summarized in the *Catechism*.

The *Catechism of the Catholic Church* "presents an organic synthesis of the essential and fundamental contents of Catholic doctrine, as regards both faith and morals, in the light of the Second Vatican Council and the whole of the Church's Tradition. Its principal sources are the Sacred Scriptures, the Fathers of the Church, the liturgy, and the Church's Magisterium. It is intended to serve 'as a point of reference for the catechisms or compendia that are composed in the various countries'" (CCC 11).

With the "eyes of faith" then, doctrines, dogmas, and propositions of faith, contained and summarized in the *Catechism*, are received not as restrictive and narrow abstractions or as burdens imposed by the Church that limit human reason and freedom. Instead the teachings of the *Catechism,* accumulated over two thousand years, are accepted as the gradual unfolding of God's loving and saving plan revealed in human history. In receiving the teachings of the Church, as proposed in the *Catechism,* one is truly free to accept and live by the truth that comes from God.

Every Church dogma and Church doctrine takes on its fullest meaning only when understood in the light of our relationship with God in Jesus Christ by the power of the Holy Spirit. The authority of the Church in proposing doctrines and dogmas contained in the *Catechism* comes from Christ himself. For, "the Church's Magisterium exercises the authority it holds from Christ to the fullest extent when it defines dogmas, that is, when it proposes, in a form obliging the Christian people to an irrevocable adherence of faith, truths contained in divine Revelation" (CCC 88).

As part of preparing those in faith formation to receive God's word, catechists will invite openness of heart and mind to the mysteries of faith, as presented in the *Catechism*. Catechists see themselves as "servants of Christ and stewards of the mysteries of God" (1 Cor 4:1). The one being catechized is introduced to truths contained in the *Catechism* as first principles of faith, derived from divine Revelation and transmitted through Sacred Scripture and Sacred Tradition. Without these first principles of faith derived from divine Revelation, the catechist is like the science teacher who sets out to teach physics without reference to the fundamental principles of physics.

The doctrines or dogmas of faith are proposed not as burdensome or restrictive. Rather, they provide a compass for the spiritual journey, and offer "lights along the path of faith; they illuminate it and make it secure … if our life is upright, our intellect and heart will be open to welcome the light shed by the dogmas of faith" (CCC 89). The Church invites each baptized Catholic to "re-appropriate exact knowledge of the faith, so as to reinvigorate it, purify it, confirm it, and confess it." [94]

Affirming that the content of catechesis is derived from divine Revelation presupposes that each catechist will select and adapt catechetical methodologies best suited to those being formed in faith. Yet without the starting point of foundational principles of faith the content of faith formation can quickly be reduced to the catechist's personal opinions or thinly disguised values of a secular culture, rather than the life-giving message of the Gospel. Catechists of the new evangelization should avoid the "temptation to mix catechetical teaching unduly with overt or masked ideological views, especially political and social ones, or with personal political opinions. When such views get the better of the central message to be transmitted, to the point of obscuring it and putting it in second place or even using it to further their own ends, catechesis then becomes radically distorted." [95]

To be human is to hold to a set of beliefs that guide one's daily life, actions, decisions and relationships. The *Catechism* presents to us the fundamental content of Catholic belief, worship, the moral life, and prayer, in response to this basic human need. Catechists in the new evangelization will help those in faith formation to recognize that the truths of the Catechism conveyed to us in the form of doctrines, dogmas, and propositions, are in fact the lights by which the Christian disciple sees the world, the light that illumines the eyes to see humbly and clearly all of God's creation and to respond in faith to the divine desire for union and friendship with humanity.

Pope Benedict reflects on the "profound unity between the act by which we believe and the content to which we give our assent in faith" when he writes,

> The heart indicates that the first act by which one comes to faith is God's gift and the action of grace which acts and transforms the person deep within … knowing the content to be believed is not sufficient unless the heart, the authentic sacred space within the person, is opened by grace that allows the eyes to see below the surface and to understand that what has been proclaimed is the word of God … A Christian may never think of belief as a private act. Faith is choosing to stand with the Lord so as to live with him. This "standing with him" points towards an understanding of the reasons for believing.[96]

Questions for Reflection and Discussion

1. Identify common difficulties or obstacles to the reception of the teachings of the Church, as contained in the *Catechism*, you encounter in adult faith formation.

   _____

   _____

   _____

2. Discuss practical ways to help adults you catechize to overcome obstacles to reading and understanding the content of faith, as presented in the *Catechism*.

   _____

   _____

   _____

3. Identify concrete ways to invite openness of heart and mind to the content of catechesis, as summarized in the *Catechism*.

   _____

   _____

   _____

> Catechesis will always draw its content from the living source of the Word of God transmitted in Tradition and the Scriptures, for "sacred Tradition and Sacred Scripture make up a single sacred deposit of the Word of God, which is entrusted to the Church."
>
> Blessed Pope John Paul II,
> *On Catechesis in our Time*, 27

2. The *Catechism of the Catholic Church*, its origin and purpose

The *Catechism of the Catholic Church*, published some twenty years ago, stands in a long line of catechisms that trace back to the earliest centuries of the Church's existence. During the first four to five centuries of Christianity there quickly arose the need for authentic and complete summaries of Christian faith. These summaries of Christian belief were called "professions of faith" or "creeds" from the first word contained in them: *credo* or "I believe." As the *Catechism* notes, "from the beginning, the apostolic Church expressed and handed on her faith in brief formulae for all. But already early on, the Church also wanted to gather the essential elements of its faith into organic and articulated summaries, intended especially for candidates for Baptism" (CCC 186). There has never been a time when the fundamental tenets of Christian faith were not condensed into creeds or other summary forms that presented the essentials of Christian faith. While the earliest summaries of faith primarily took the form of creeds, as time went on, they gradually expanded to include the Church's essential doctrines on the Sacraments, the Christian moral life, and prayer. Over the centuries, various universal catechisms have presented the essentials of the Catholic faith following the traditional catechetical order of Creed, Sacraments, the Christian Moral Life, and Prayer.

History of the *Catechism of the Catholic Church*

The Church marks the twentieth anniversary of the publication of the *Catechism of the Catholic Church* in 2012. In renewing our appreciation for this treasure of faith we recognize that this universal *Catechism* is, first and foremost, "both an authentic fruit of Vatican Council II and a tool for aiding in its reception."[97] On almost every page of the *Catechism* one finds references and cross-references, quotes, and explanations of the teachings contained in the sixteen documents of the Second Vatican Council. As we strive to understand the teachings of the Second Vatican Council, it can be said the *Catechism of the Catholic Church* provides an authentic interpretation of that conciliar event and its documents.

In January 1985, Blessed Pope John Paul II convoked an Extraordinary Assembly of the Synod of Bishops to mark the twentieth anniversary of the closing of the Second Vatican Council. On that occasion, many bishops expressed the need and desire for a universal "Catechism or compendium of Catholic doctrine regarding both faith and morals be composed, that it might be, as it were, a point of reference for catechisms or compendiums that are prepared in various regions" (Blessed Pope John Paul II, *Fidei Depositum*).

An extensive process of collaboration followed over six years as the work of preparing the text of the *Catechism* unfolded. The text of the *Catechism* was carefully drafted under the direction of a Commission of twelve Cardinals and Bishops, chaired by then Cardinal Joseph Ratzinger, and supported by an editorial committee of seven diocesan Bishops, who were assisted by experts in theology and catechesis. The *Catechism*, as we have it today, was the result of extensive collaboration among the Bishops of the world, and of responses from theological and catechetical institutes. As Blessed Pope John Paul II observed, "This response elicits in me a deep feeling of joy, because the harmony of so many voices truly expresses what could be called the 'symphony' of the faith. The achievement of this *Catechism* thus reflects the collegial nature of the Episcopate; it testifies to the Church's catholicity" (*Fidei Depositum*, 1). In the twenty years since its publication and largely positive reception, the *Catechism* has borne rich fruit in the lives of the faithful. Its consistent use in faith formation also contributes to a gradual renewal of catechesis and supports ongoing catechist formation.

The content of the universal *Catechism* includes "the new and the old, because the faith is always the same yet the source of ever new light." In its structure this *Catechism* follows the previous universal catechisms in the arrangement of content into four parts or "pillars":

- One, the *Creed* (what the Church believes in faith);
- Two, the *Sacred Liturgy*, with expositions on the seven Sacraments (how the Church celebrates her faith);
- Three, the *Christian way of life* explained by way of the Ten Commandments and the Beatitudes (how the Church responds to the commands of love in a complete way of life); and
- Four, *Christian Prayer* (how the life of Christian faith is deepened and nourished).

Discovering the inner unity and relationship between the four "pillars" or sections of the *Catechism* is a vital part of unfolding its riches. As Blessed Pope John Paul II noted while introducing the *Catechism* to the world:

> The four parts are related to one another; the Christian mystery is the object of faith (first part); it is celebrated and communicated in liturgical actions (second part); it is present to enlighten and sustain the children of God in their actions (third part); it is the basis for our prayer, the privileged expression of which is the Our Father ... (fourth part) ... in reading the *Catechism of the Catholic Church* we can perceive the wonderful unity of the mystery of God ... as well as the central place of Jesus Christ, the only-begotten Son of God, sent by the Father, made man in the womb of the Blessed Virgin Mary by the power of the Holy Spirit, to be our Savior. Having died and risen, Christ is always present in his Church, especially in the sacraments; he is the source of our faith, the model of Christian conduct, and the Teacher of our prayer. [98]

The content of the faith "receives its systematic and organic synthesis in the *Catechism of the Catholic Church*."[99] Its purpose in the life of the Church and in the lives of each baptized Christian was summarized by Pope Benedict XVI as he proposed the celebration of a Year of Faith:

> It is in this sense that the Year of Faith will have to see a concerted effort to rediscover and study the fundamental content of the faith that receives its systematic and organic synthesis in the *Catechism of the Catholic Church*. Here, in fact, we see the wealth of teaching that the Church has received, safeguarded and proposed in her two thousand years of history. From Sacred Scripture to the Fathers of the Church, from theological masters to the saints across the centuries, the *Catechism* provides a permanent record of the many ways in which the Church has meditated on the faith and made progress in doctrine so as to offer certitude to believers in their lives of faith. [100]

> Faith is not the result of human effort, of human reasoning, but rather a gift of God ... Faith starts with God, who opens his heart to us and invites us to share in his own divine life. Faith does not simply provide information about who Christ is; rather, it entails a personal relationship with Christ, a surrender of our whole person, with all our understanding, will and feelings, to God's self-revelation.
>
> Pope Benedict XVI, words at the beginning of the Eucharistic Celebration, 26th World Youth Day, Madrid, August 21, 2011

3. Ten "best practices" to guide the use of the *Catechism of the Catholic Church* at the service of the new evangelization

As a treasure and a gift, as a compass and light for the journey of faith, the *Catechism* is received by catechists and evangelists as a "sure norm for teaching the faith and a valid and legitimate instrument for ecclesial communion."[101] As a catechist who serves as a "steward of the mysteries of God" discovers or re-discovers the riches contained in the *Catechism* and places it at the service of faith formation in the new evangelization, the following "best practices" for its use are offered for discussion and reflection.

These "best practices" assume that a catechist is open to drawing with confidence and with charity on the mysteries and truths of faith summarized in the *Catechism*. As the sure catechetical reference point and authoritative source for the content of faith formation, a catechist receives the *Catechism* in humility, joy, and with gratitude. Since, "catechesis is a moment or aspect of evangelization, its content cannot be anything else but the content of evangelization as a whole. The one message — the Good News of salvation — that has been heard once or hundreds of times and has been accepted with the heart, is in catechesis probed unceasingly by reflection and systematic study, by awareness of its repercussions on one's personal life ... and by inserting it into an organic and harmonious whole, namely Christian living in society and the world." [102]

1. Make it a priority to familiarize yourself with the teachings of the *Catechism*.
While it is true that a catechist cannot pass on to others what he or she does not

have, it has also been said that a catechist passes on what he or she does not have! Familiarity with both the content and language of faith, as presented in the *Catechism,* is a first and needed step for a catechist to gain confidence in its use in the new evangelization. Do not be intimidated by the *Catechism's* theological language, or its comprehensive content. Through sustained study and reflection the depth and breadth of its teachings will unfold gradually in the mind and heart that is open to its riches. While group reading and discussion on key sections of the *Catechism* may form an essential component of catechist formation, there is no substitute for personal study and reflection on relevant sections of the *Catechism* in preparation for each catechetical session. A catechist returns time and time again to the content of the *Catechism,* while drawing on the abundant catechetical resources offered by catechetical publishers in this country. For some fifteen years, the Bishops of the United States have reviewed catechetical materials for conformity with the *Catechism*, and publish a Conformity List that identifies such reviewed catechetical resources.[103] These catechetical resources provide catechists with age appropriate and methodologically appropriate catechesis, based on the essential content of faith presented in the *Catechism*. One particularly insightful resource is the four-volume *Pillars of Faith* series by Msgr. Peter J. Vaghi, which treats each of the four pillars of the *Catechism*.

From a catechist's familiarity with the teachings of the *Catechism* flows joyful confidence in its certainty and truth. Such joyful conviction in the faith of the Church accompanies a catechist as he or she introduces and explains key catechetical themes, such as divine Revelation, Sacred Scripture, Creation, the Fall, the Trinity, the Incarnation, the Church, Mary, Mother of God, the Sacraments, the Ten Commandments and the Beatitudes, and the traditions of Christian prayer. Familiarity with the *Catechism* allows a catechist to draw readily and freely on its teachings in the catechetical setting and in the classroom. Those you catechize will grow in familiarity with the *Catechism* as a consequence of your own familiarity with its teachings. From time to time, it may be helpful to pause and discuss the need for the *Catechism* and the life-giving power of the Church's teachings, doctrines, and dogmas.

2. Pray for the inspiration of the Holy Spirit to understand, to interiorize, to share, and to live the faith contained in the *Catechism*. Approach the *Catechism* in a spirit of humble openness and willingness to be formed in thinking and acting "with the mind of the Church." Adapt the prayerfulness and silent receptivity of the practice of *lectio divina* to your reading of the *Catechism*. With humble reliance on the help and grace of the Holy Spirit a catechist's study and catechetical use of the *Catechism* will bear the rich fruit of understanding and renewed enthusiasm to witness to and live the Catholic faith. Remind those you catechize of the importance of praying for and relying on the interior help of the Holy Spirit, the "primary agent of the new evangelization,"[104] who alone enlightens the mind, opens the heart in conversion, and directs our actions and thoughts to love of God and love of neighbor.

The Holy Spirit is the soul of the Church. It is He who explains to the faithful the deep meaning of the teaching of Jesus and His Mystery.... It is the Holy Spirit who, just as at the beginning of the Church, acts in every evangelizer ... techniques of evangelization are good, but even the most advanced ones could not replace the gentle action of the Holy Spirit. The most perfect preparation of the evangelizer has no effect without the Holy Spirit ... if the Spirit of God has a preeminent place in the whole life of the Church, it is in her evangelizing mission that He is most active.

Pope Paul VI, *Evangelii Nuntiandi*, 75

3. Lead others to Jesus Christ who stands at the center and heart of the *Catechism*. Every page and every teaching of the *Catechism* leads to and expresses the living faith of the Church as a graced encounter with the Person of Jesus Christ. It is Christ who stands at the heart of every page of the *Catechism*. When the teachings of the *Catechism* are presented as a means to learning and understanding better the life, death, and Resurrection of the Lord, it becomes more readily accessible, less abstract or intimidating to those in faith formation. The challenge for a catechist is to relate continually each particular teaching in the *Catechism* to the whole of Jesus' life and saving mission. For as Blessed Pope John Paul II reminded catechists:

At the heart of catechesis we find, in essence, a Person, the Person of Jesus of Nazareth, the only Son from the Father.... To catechize is to reveal in the Person of Christ the whole of God's eternal design reaching fulfillment in that Person. It is to seek to understand the meaning of Christ's actions and words and of the signs worked by him." Catechesis aims at putting people ... in communion with Jesus Christ; only He can lead us to the love of the Father in the Spirit and make us share in the life of the Holy Trinity.[105]

In using the *Catechism* as a point of reference, a catechist makes sure to connect the "*what*" of faith to "*how*" faith is expressed concretely in the "art of living" as a disciple of Jesus Christ. The catechist takes up the task of "translating" the teachings of the *Catechism* so that they are received, not as abstractions or impositions, but as encounters with the Person of Jesus Christ who reconciles us to friendship with God and with one another. As Pope Benedict XVI has observed,

In its very structure, the *Catechism of the Catholic Church* follows the development of the faith right up to the great themes of daily life. On page after page, we find that what is presented here is no theory, but an encounter with a Person who lives within the Church. The profession of faith is followed by an account of the sacramental life, in which Christ is present, operative and continues to build his Church. Without the liturgy and Sacraments, the profession of faith would lack efficacy, because it would lack the grace which supports Christian witness. By the same criterion, the teaching of the *Catechism* on the moral life acquires its full meaning if placed in relationship with faith, liturgy, and prayer.[106]

4. Avoid setting catechetical content against catechetical methods. In preparation for each catechetical session a catechist resists the tendency to set catechetical content against catechetical method. It is a false dichotomy to set in opposition the one content of faith, as presented in the *Catechism,* against the multiplicity of catechetical methods used to communicate the truths of faith. In the words of Blessed Pope John Paul II:

> It is useless to play off orthopraxis against orthodoxy. Christianity is inseparably both … it is also quite useless to campaign for the abandonment of serious and orderly study of the message of Christ in the name of a method concentrating solely on life experience. "No one can arrive at the whole truth on the basis solely of some simple private experience, that is to say, without an adequate explanation of the message of Christ, who is "the Way, the Truth, and the Life" (John 14:6). Nor is any opposition to be set up between a catechesis taking life as its point of departure and a traditional doctrinal and systematic catechesis. Authentic catechesis is always an orderly and systematic initiation into the revelation that God has given of Himself to humanity in Christ Jesus, a revelation stored in the depths of the Church's memory and in Sacred Scripture, and constantly communicated from one generation to the next by a living, active *traditio.* This revelation is not however isolated from life or artificially juxtaposed to it. It is concerned with the ultimate meaning of life and it illumines the whole of life with the light of the Gospel, to inspire it or to question it. [107]

In attending to the content of catechesis a catechist also distinguishes between presenting the "text" of the *Catechism* on the one hand, and his or her own "commentary," on the other hand. Here the "text" refers not only to the actual words of the *Catechism,* but includes its meaning and sense. This distinction in presenting the teachings of the *Catechism* is important since "every baptized person, precisely by reason of being baptized, has the right to receive from the Church instruction and education enabling him or her to enter into a truly Christian life." [108] Then Cardinal Joseph Ratzinger once observed:

> This distinction among various levels (is) extremely important … (and) the fact that instructors have forgotten the difference between "text" and "commentary." The text, that is to say, the actual content of what has to be said, progressively disappeared in the commentary, but in that way the commentary no longer had anything to comment on. It became its own standard and thus lost its seriousness … the *Roman Catechism's* distinction between the basic text of the proclamation of the faith and the spoken or written texts by which it is imparted is by no means just one didactic path among other possible methods; rather it is an essential part of the matter. [109]

A catechist has a duty to maintain the integrity of the content of catechesis since the "person who becomes a disciple of Christ has the right to receive the word of faith not in mutilated, falsified or diminished form but whole and entire, in all its rigor and vigor. Unfaithfulness on some point to the integrity of the message means a dangerous weakening of catechesis and putting at risk the results that Christ and the ecclesial community have a right to expect from it ... no true catechist can lawfully, on his own initiative, make a selection of what he considers important in the deposit of faith as opposed to what he considers unimportant, so as to teach the one and reject the other." [110]

To effectively advance the new evangelization a catechist will employ those catechetical methods that serve best the content of catechesis. The "pedagogy of God" or the "divine pedagogy" (see *General Directory for Catechesis*, Part III) guides the discernment and selection of catechetical methods that serve to convey the meaning contained in the sources of divine Revelation in Sacred Scripture and Sacred Tradition. The varieties of catechetical methods, determined by age appropriateness, intellectual capacity, developmental readiness, cultural context, and spiritual maturity, all point to the richness and unity of the content of faith.

5. Don't stop at presenting the formulas of faith contained in the *Catechism*.
The teachings of the Catholic faith contained in the *Catechism* are condensed into brief formulas and propositions of faith. Theological language developed over centuries may not be readily or easily understood at first. In fact, every paragraph of the *Catechism*, in one way or another, condenses some two thousand years of the apostolic faith of the Catholic Church. Lead those you catechize to reflect on the divine mysteries of faith that are conveyed and expressed in the formulas of faith contained in the *Catechism*. For "we do not believe in formulas, but in those realities they express, which faith allows us to touch" (CCC 170).

Remember that the formulas and propositions of faith point to sacred mysteries and divinely revealed realities, accepted in faith. In drawing on the *Catechism* in the catechetical setting or classroom, remind your students that the formulas and propositions of faith always point to the living mystery of God revealed in Jesus Christ in the power of the Holy Spirit. While we approach these mysteries of faith with the help of propositions "which permit us to express the faith and to hand it on, to celebrate it in community, to assimilate and live on it more and more," (CCC 170), the formulas of faith are not the final objective of catechesis. To stop at the formulas and propositions of faith is to miss the point entirely, since they are meant as guideposts leading us into the "art of living" as a disciple of Jesus Christ in His Body, the Church.

6. Relate the content of the *Catechism* to the lives of the saints and to your own personal witness to faith.
The "communion of saints" witness to the faith of the Church as it is lived in every age, culture, and place. Through a living "theology of holiness," the saints show by the examples of their lives that it is indeed possible for the content of catechesis to

be accepted and to be lived to the full. In the lives of the saints, faith and life come together. To unpack the teachings of the *Catechism* in light of the lives of the saints and your own personal witness to living faith serves to counter the secular view that faith is simply a matter of private superstition or piety. Your personal witness to how your profession of faith in the Creed is nourished and strengthened through full participation in the Church's sacraments, lived in the Christian moral life and deepened through prayer relates the *Catechism* to a lived experience of Christian discipleship. As one author writes, "Remember, you are the only church some people may ever visit!" [111]

It may be easy to dispute one or another point of doctrine presented in the *Catechism,* but it is hard to argue with the witness of a Christian saint or disciple whose entire life radiates the life-changing truth, power, and beauty of faith in Jesus Christ. The lives of the saints, in particular, offer a lived evangelizing and inculturated catechesis. By relating a particular truth of the *Catechism* to the example of a saintly man or woman a catechist, in effect, incarnates and inculturates the content of faith in the experiential dimensions of daily life. An outstanding example of this "best practice" is to be found in the *United States Catholic Catechism for Adults* (USCCA), in which each chapter begins with the life of one American saintly figure who represents a living, joyful, and fully human witness to Christian faith.

7. Remember the "analogy of faith" (CCC 114) and the "hierarchy of truths" (CCC 90) that point to the coherence of the teachings of the *Catechism* with one another and within the whole plan of God's revelation. As a catechist becomes familiar with its content, the *Catechism* unfolds as a harmonious "symphony of faith" in the inter-relatedness of beliefs, worship, moral life, and prayer. The source of this unity in the *Catechism* is not in our human ingenuity or creativity. Rather its inner coherence and its hierarchy of truths originate in God's single and loving plan of salvation, attested to in Sacred Scripture and in Sacred Tradition. No truth of faith contained in the *Catechism* stands alone. Rather one mystery of faith is illuminated from within by another mystery of faith that sheds mutual light, and confirms and deepens its meaning and application to daily life. The in-brief sections of the Catechism, the cross-references in the margins, and the numerous footnotes on each page are excellent sources that point to the inner coherence and unity of the entire *Catechism*.

As a catechist points to the mutual connections that exist between the articles of the Creed and the seven Sacraments, and relates how the Christian moral life is strengthened through sacramental graces and supported through prayer, the beauty of the Catholic faith begins to radiate from the whole *Catechism*. For "the mutual connections between dogmas, and their coherence, can be found in the whole of the Revelation of the mystery of Christ.… 'In Catholic doctrine there exists an order or "hierarchy" of truths, since they vary in their relation to the foundations of the Christian faith'" (CCC 90).

8. Draw on the content of the *Catechism* to respond to challenges to the Catholic faith.

No catechist is exempt from fielding questions, doubts, and even objections to the Catholic faith. In proposing the Gospel anew, catechists will eventually be called to respond to misunderstandings, reservations, or outright rejection of the tenets of the Catholic faith. Through open and honest dialogue there may be times when questions, objections, and doubts lead to deeper understanding, stronger convictions, and renewed commitment to active participation in the Church's life. At other times, a catechist may be overwhelmed or feel ill prepared to adequately respond to persistent objections, misperceptions, or cultural barriers to acceptance of the Gospel. This may happen especially when presenting moral principles, such as Catholic truths on the dignity of every human life, the sacredness of human sexuality and chastity, and marriage as the union of one man and one woman.

In answering objections to the teachings of the Catholic Church, shape your responses through a careful and prayerful reading and meditation on the *Catechism*. Pause to ask yourself: How is this particular difficulty, challenge, question, or doubt answered directly or indirectly in the content of faith, as presented in the *Catechism*? Remember that while you may be familiar with the reasons that support a particular teaching of the Church, these reasons may be completely new or difficult to grasp for someone in faith formation who may be hearing it for the first time. Be patient with those who may be slow to comprehend or accept the mysteries of faith, recognizing that each person is on a unique spiritual and intellectual path of conversion.

In his treatise *On Christian Doctrine*, Saint Augustine urged his catechists to witness to the faith so as to "cultivate delight" in faith. He used the familiar experience of taking a friend on a tour of a place of interest that they have never seen before. The tour guide has passed by the place often and knows it well enough that it is routine. But now he finds his own delight renewed by the delight of the visitors for whom it is all new. In the same way, a catechist is renewed in faith as the one being catechized comes to faith anew and with delight, by seeing for the first time through the "eyes of faith."

The task of the catechist is to form and teach others faithfully, clearly, and with the love of God. Be confident to speak the truth in love, with the assurance that the Holy Spirit is the one who opens the hearts and minds of those you catechize. The mysteries of faith are proposed, never imposed on the mind and heart. Recall that the minds and hearts of those we catechize are often more convinced by the inherent reasonableness and beauty of faith and the graces contained in each truth of faith, rather than by mere human eloquence or cleverness on our part. A catechist's own humble, joyful, and loving acceptance of even the most difficult to understand and accept truths of faith is in itself a compelling witness to its truth and power. Cardinal Edouard Gagnon once shared an insight he gained from a conversation with Blessed Pope John Paul II about the difficulties inherent in proposing the Gospel:

The Pope told me, "Error makes its way because truth is not taught. We must teach the truth, repeat it, not attacking the ones who teach errors, because that would never end-they are so numerous. We have to teach the truth." He told me that truth has a grace attached to it. Anytime we speak the truth, we conform to what Christ teaches and what is being taught by the Church. Every time we stand up for the truth, there is an internal grace from God that accompanies that truth. The truth may not immediately enter into the mind and heart of those to whom we talk, but the grace of God is there and at the time they need it, God will open their heart and they will accept it. He said that error does not have grace accompanying it. It might have all the external means, but it does not have the grace of God accompanying it. This encouraged me very much. [112]

9. Encourage family catechesis as the place where the Catechism is read, discussed, and reflected on in an ongoing way beyond the catechetical setting or classroom. We are reminded that "family catechesis precedes, accompanies, and enriches all other forms of catechesis." [113] As members of the family help each other to grow in faith through the witness of a Christian life in the "domestic Church," that is a Christian home, the *Catechism* serves as a sure point of reference for parents who are the "primary educators in the faith" of their children. Catechesis in the new evangelization will find invaluable support and enrichment from the witness of Christian families in the home, in their neighborhoods and communities, and in society. Since "the family is also the primary place for evangelization, for passing on the faith, for helping young people to appreciate the importance of religious practice and Sunday observance." [114] Ongoing reflection and discussion on faith formation received in the catechetical setting and classroom extends into the home as children share catechetical reflections with their parents, and adults join with their spouses and children to reflect on God's word each Sunday and on the content of faith throughout the Church's liturgical seasons. Through selection of catechetical activities that directly or indirectly engage the family in reflection and discussion on the teachings of the *Catechism,* a catechist encourages and fosters family catechesis.

10. The law of love permeates every catechetical presentation of the *Catechism.* We have reflected on the "apologetics of love" in chapter two. Here we simply affirm, once again, the priority and primacy of Christian love in the use of the *Catechism* in catechetical settings. This witness to love of God and love of neighbor takes root first in the catechist's own love for God and neighbor. The catechist's own love for the faith of the Church becomes the motivation and inspiration of all catechetical instruction and witness to the content of the *Catechism.* A catechist discovers that the most credible and compelling reason for every reality of faith conveyed in the *Catechism* is the love of God revealed through His Son Jesus Christ who reconciles humanity to Himself. For this reason, Saint Augustine would even go so far as to encourage catechists in his day to approach catechizing with "a brother's, a father's, and a mother's love."

Friendship with Jesus will also lead you to bear witness to the faith wherever you are, even when it meets with rejection or indifference. We cannot encounter Christ and not want to make him known to others. So do not keep Christ to yourselves! Share with others the joy of your faith. The world needs the witness of your faith, it surely needs God…. You too have been given the extraordinary task of being disciples and missionaries of Christ.

Pope Benedict XVI, words at the beginning of the Eucharistic Celebration, 26th World Youth Day, Madrid, August 21, 2011

Without this Christian witness to love of God and love of neighbor, a catechist's presentation of the teachings of the *Catechism* is quickly reduced to abstract and remote formulas that may or may not have immediate relevance to daily life or have cultural resonance. Without a catechist's witness to Christian love the teachings of faith easily appear burdensome and as impositions from without. Misunderstandings, doubts, and rejection of faith easily follow. Through study, discussion, and reception of the *Catechism* a person is to encounter nothing less than divine love that alone transforms, converts, and saves.

The *Catechism* (CCC 25) highlights this primacy and priority of love in catechetical ministry when it recalls this pastoral principle of the *Roman Catechism*:

> The whole concern of doctrine and its teachings must be directed to the love that never ends. Whether something is proposed for belief, for hope or for action, the love of our Lord must always be made accessible, so that anyone can see that all the works of perfect Christian virtue spring from love and have no other objective than to arrive at love.

Questions for Reflection and Discussion

1. Share concrete ways in which you will take up anew the *Catechism of the Catholic Church* as a treasure of faith and a catechetical tool that serves the new evangelization.

2. Why is the "analogy of faith" and the "hierarchy of truths" in the *Catechism* to be considered in drawing on its riches in catechetical ministry?

3. Identify concrete steps you can take to familiarize yourself with the content of the *Catechism*.

_____

_____

4. Discuss examples of catechetical activities that promote family catechesis that are inspired by the *Catechism*.

_____

_____

5. Share actual ways in which your catechetical instruction and personal witness to faith can be further inspired by the priority of the "law of love" in catechesis.

_____

_____

Conclusion

1. Mary, Star of the New Evangelization

As we conclude our reflections on the use of the *Catechism of the Catholic Church* at the service of the new evangelization we look to the Blessed Virgin Mary, Mother of God and Mother of the Church. For more than two thousand years, the Catholic Church has honored the Virgin Mary under various titles and names. The rich variety of Marian titles and names is itself an expression of the evangelization of diverse cultures and languages.

Blessed Pope John Paul II encouraged the faithful to turn to the intercession of Mary under the title, "Star of the New Evangelization." At the dawn of the third Christian millennium he wrote, "I have often invoked her as the 'Star of the New Evangelization.' Now I point to Mary once again as the radiant dawn and sure guide for our steps. Once more, echoing the words of Jesus himself and giving voice to the filial affection of the whole Church, I say to her: 'Woman, behold your children' (John 19:26)" (*Novo Millennio Ineunte*, 58).

At the Annunciation, Mary receives the message of the angel Gabriel in humility and in trust. In her "yes," her "*fiat*," to God's word, Mary gives her consent to the Incarnation and uniquely cooperates in the saving plan of God for the salvation of the world. In her actions, thoughts, and throughout her life, Mary ponders the mystery of the Word made flesh and points us, her children in faith, to her divine Son as the Redeemer of the world.

Catechists and evangelists look to Mary, Star of the New Evangelization, for her example and her maternal intercession. Like the Blessed Virgin Mary, catechists who serve the new evangelization ponder continually the Word of God in their heart. Through an evangelizing and inculturated catechesis her Son, Jesus Christ, is made present in the world through word and deed, proclamation and witness. As Mother of the Church and our mother in the order of faith, Mary prepares, guides, and strengthens every catechist to open the door of faith so that others may come to know, love, and live the new life of grace in her Son Jesus, the true light and Redeemer of the world.

2. The miracle of the new evangelization

A reflection on the cover art by Jacopo Bassano, *The Miraculous Draught of Fishes*, 1545, National Gallery of Art, Washington, D.C., oil on canvas

Jesus tells his disciples to "go therefore and make disciples of all nations, baptizing them in the name of the Father and of the Son and of the Holy Spirit, teaching them to observe all that I commanded you" (Matthew 29:19–20). As the apostles spread out into the known world to make known the "Good News" of the saving death and Resurrection of the Lord they extend this evangelizing mandate of Jesus to the ends of the earth.

The Gospel account of the miraculous catch of fish is depicted in a dramatic sixteenth century painting by the Venetian artist Jacopo Bassano entitled, *The Miraculous Draught of Fishes*. The scene is described for us in the opening verses of the fifth chapter of Saint Luke's Gospel (5:1–11). The account begins with Jesus who is standing by the lake of Gennesaret where he sees two empty boats. He steps into one of the boats, which belonged to Simon, and asked the disciple to pull away from the shore. After teaching the people from the boat, he turns to Simon and says, "Put out into the deep and let your nets down for a catch" (v. 4). Simon responds that the disciples have been toiling all night and have not been successful. He goes on to say to Jesus, "But at your word I will let down the nets." Saint Luke then tells us that when the disciples let down their nets they brought in a shoal of fish so large that their nets were at breaking point.

Jacopo Bassano captures each vivid detail of this Gospel account in his masterful composition. We see the strong figure of Jesus seated in the boat as he raises one hand in the gesture of a teacher. As Saint Luke recounts, after the miraculous catch of fish Simon kneels in awe at Jesus' feet saying, "Depart from me, for I am a sinful man, Lord" (v. 8). The apostle Andrew stands at the center of the scene and also expresses his amazement at the miracle that has just unfolded before their eyes.

On the right side of the painting, we see Zebedee and his sons James and John as they strain to pull the breaking nets. A few struggling fish break the water's surface. Both groups of disciples are united around the dramatic green cape of the apostle Andrew that flutters across the sweeping winds. Bassano's use of brilliant colors of rose red, orange, and green in the foreground radiate across the pale blue waters and sky in the landscape background. All of the dramatic expressions of the disciples lead one's eye to the powerful figure of Jesus as he brings about this miracle while saying to Simon, "Do not be afraid, henceforth you will be fishers of men."

This image from the National Gallery of Art in Washington, D.C., was chosen for the book cover for several reasons. For one, it points to the central mystery of the person of Jesus Christ in the new evangelization. It also serves as a visual reminder that all new evangelization efforts share in the miracle of the disciples' abundant catch to the extent that the Lord's call to "put out into the deep" is heard and lived. At first our evangelizing and catechetical efforts may not meet with much "success," just as the disciples complain, "we have worked hard all night and have caught nothing." It is only when Simon Peter obeys the Lord's command and says, "Master, at your word I will let down the nets," that the miraculous catch of fish occurs. Jesus' call to Simon gives deep confidence to the disciples to overcome their doubts and fears. His words to Simon, "Do not be afraid," are addressed to us as well as we each take our part in the new evangelization. We are reminded that the

"success" of all of the Church's evangelizing and catechetical efforts depend always on our attentive hearing and doing of God's word. As Pope Benedict XVI has noted:

> Today too, the Church and the successors of the Apostles are told to put out into the deep sea of history and to let down the nets, so to win men and women over to the Gospel — to God, to Christ, to true life … we are living in alienation, in the salt waters of suffering and death; in a sea of darkness without light. The net of the Gospel pulls us out of the waters of death and brings us into the splendor of God's light, into true life. It is really true: as we follow Christ in this mission to be fishers of men, we must bring men and women out of the sea that is salted with so many forms of alienation and onto the land of life, into the light of God. It is really so: the purpose of our lives is to reveal God to men. And only where God is seen does life truly begin. Only when we meet the living God in Christ do we know what life is … the task of the fisher of men can often seem wearisome. But it is beautiful and wonderful, because it is truly a service to joy, to God's joy which longs to break into the world. (Pope Benedict XVI, Homily at the Mass for the Beginning of the Petrine Ministry of the Bishop of Rome, April 24, 2005)

Notes

1   Joseph Cardinal Ratzinger, "On the New Evangelization," Address to Catechists and Religion Teachers, Jubilee for Catechists, December 12, 2000, Rome.

2   *Lineamenta* for the Synod of Bishops, XIII Ordinary General Assembly on the New Evangelization for the Transmission of the Christian Faith.

3   Rodney Stark, The Rise of Christianity: *How the Obscure, Marginal Jesus Movement Became the Dominant Religious Force in the Western World*, Princeton University Press, 1966, 208.

4   Pope John XXIII, Apostolic Constitution, *Humanae Salutis* (Convocation of the Second Vatican Council), December 25, 1961, Rome.

5   Pope John XXIII, Opening Speech to the Council, October 11, 1962, Rome.

6   Pope Paul VI, Apostolic Exhortation, *Evangelii Nuntiandi* (December 8, 1975), 18, 26 and 27.

7   Blessed Pope John Paul II, *Crossing the Threshold of Hope*, 1994.

8   Blessed Pope John Paul II, Opening Address to the 6th General Assembly of CELAM (Latin American Episcopal Council), March 9, 1983, Port-au-Prince, Haiti.

9   Pope Benedict XVI, Homily on the Solemnity of the Holy Apostles Peter and Paul, June 28, 2010.

10 *Lineamenta* for the Synod of Bishops, XIII Ordinary General Assembly on The New Evangelization for the Transmission of the Christian Faith, 23.

11 Cardinal Donald Wuerl, *Disciples of the Lord: Sharing the Vision*, Pastoral Letter on the New Evangelization, September 8, 2010.

12 Pope Benedict XVI, Homily at Saint Patrick's Cathedral, New York, Saturday, April 18, 2008.

13 Pope Benedict XVI, Apostolic Letter (Motu Proprio), *Porta Fidei*, 7.

14 Joseph Cardinal Ratzinger, "On the New Evangelization," Address to Catechists and Religion Teachers, Jubilee for Catechists, December 12, 2000, Rome.

15 *Lineamenta* for the Synod of Bishops, XIII Ordinary General Assembly on The New Evangelization for the Transmission of the Christian Faith.

16 Second Vatican Council II, Dogmatic Constitution, *Lumen Gentium*, 1.

17 Blessed Pope John Paul II, *On the Coming Third Millennium, Tertio Millenio Adveniente*, 6

18 Cardinal Donald Wuerl, *Disciples of the Lord: Sharing the Vision*, Pastoral Letter on the New Evangelization, September 8, 2010.

19 Blessed Pope John Paul II, On Catechesis In Our Time, *Catechesi Tradendae* (1979), 6.

20 Blessed Pope John Paul II, On Catechesis In Our Time, *Catechesi Tradendae*, (1979), 9.

21 Second Vatican Council II, The Constitution on the Sacred Liturgy, *Sacrosanctum Concilium*, 14.

22 Blessed Pope John Paul II, *Redemptoris Missio*, 21-30.

23 Blessed Pope John Paul II, Homily for the Beatification of Mother Teresa on World Mission Sunday.

24 Joseph Cardinal Ratzinger, "On the New Evangelization," Address to Catechists and Religion Teachers, Jubilee for Catechists, December 12, 2000, Rome.

25 *Lineamenta* for the Synod of Bishops, XIII Ordinary General Assembly on The New Evangelization for the Transmission of the Christian Faith, 2.

26 Pope Paul VI, *Evangelii Nuntiani*, 75

27 Congregation for the Doctrine of the Faith, Doctrinal Note on Some Aspects of Evangelization, December 2007.

28 Joseph Cardinal Ratzinger, "On the New Evangelization," Address to Catechists and Religion Teachers, Jubilee for Catechists, December 12, 2000, Rome.

29 Joseph Cardinal Ratzinger, "On the New Evangelization," Address to Catechists and Religion Teachers, Jubilee for Catechists, December 12. 2000, Rome.

30 *Catechism of the Catholic Church*, 27.

31 Joseph Cardinal Ratzinger, "On the New Evangelization," Address to Catechists and Religion Teachers, Jubilee for Catechists, December 12, 2000, Rome.

32 Joseph Cardinal Ratzinger, "On the New Evangelization," Address to Catechists and Religion Teachers, Jubilee for Catechists, December 12, 2000, Rome.

33 Joseph Cardinal Ratzinger, "On the New Evangelization," Address to Catechists and Religion Teachers, Jubilee for Catechists, December 12, 2000, Rome.

34 Joseph Cardinal Ratzinger, "On the New Evangelization," Address to Catechists and Religion Teachers, Jubilee for Catechists, December 12, 2000, Rome.

35 *Lineamenta* for the Synod of Bishops, XIII Ordinary General Assembly on The New Evangelization for the Transmission of the Christian Faith.

36 Pope Benedict XVI, Homily on the Solemnity of the Holy Apostles Peter and Paul, June 28, 2010.

37 Blessed Pope John Paul II, Address to Young People of Gniezno, Poland, June 3, 1979.

38 Joseph Cardinal Ratzinger, "On the New Evangelization," Address to Catechists and Religion Teachers, Jubilee for Catechists, December 12, 2000, Rome.

39 Blessed Pope John Paul II, Homily at Mass in Saint Louis, Pastoral Visit to United States, January 1999.

40 Blessed Pope John Paul II, On Catechesis in Our Time, *Catechesi Tradendae*, 6.

41 Pope Benedict XVI, Homily on the Solemnity of the Holy Apostles Peter and Paul, June 28, 2010.

42 Congregation for the Clergy, *General Directory for Catechesis*, 63.

43 Congregation for the Clergy, *General Directory for Catechesis*, 46.

44 Congregation for the Clergy, *General Directory for Catechesis*, 58 (c).

45 Blessed Pope John Paul II, On Catechesis in Our Time, *Catechesi Tradendae*, 20.

46 Congregation for the Clergy, *General Directory for Catechesis*, 64.

47 Congregation for the Clergy, *General Directory for Catechesis*, 61.

48 Congregation for the Clergy, *General Directory for Catechesis*, 63.

49 *Lineamenta* for the Synod of Bishops, XIII Ordinary General Assembly on The New Evangelization for the Transmission of the Christian Faith, 19.

50 Congregation for the Doctrine of the Faith, *Doctrinal Note on Some Aspects of Evangelization*, December 2007, paragraph 8.

51   Pope Benedict XVI, Homily on the Solemnity of the Holy Apostles Peter and Paul, June 28, 2010.

52   John Cavadini, presentation delivered at "The Intellectual Tasks of the New Evangelization," symposium hosted by the USCCB Committee on Doctrine, September 2011.

53   Congregation for the Doctrine of Faith, *Doctrinal Note on Some Aspects of Evangelization*, December 2007, paragraph 8 and 10.

54   Vatican Council II, Declaration on Religious Liberty, *Dignitatis Humanae*, December 7, 1965, 1, in Vatican Council II, Gen. ed. Austin Flannery, O.P., 1988 Revised edition, Saint Paul Editions.

55   Joseph Cardinal Ratzinger, "On the New Evangelization," Address to Catechists and Religion Teachers, Jubilee for Catechists, December 12, 2000, Rome.

56   Blessed Pope John Paul II, *Address to the International Council for Catechesis*, September 26, 1992 (L'Osservatore Romano, English Edition, 25/42, October 7, 1992, 5).

57   Congregation for the Clergy, *General Directory for Catechesis*, 109.

58   Congregation for the Clergy, *General Directory for Catechesis*, 109.

59   Vatican Council II, *Lumen Gentium*, 8, and *Sacrosanctum Concilium*, 2.

60   Congregation for the Clergy, *General Directory for Catechesis*, 110.

61   Pope Paul VI, Apostolic Exhortation *Evangelii Nuntiandi* (December 8, 1975), 14.

62   Father James A. Wehner, S.T.D. *The Evangelization Equation: The Who, What, and How*, Emmaus Road Publishing, 2011, page xviii.

63   Aidan Nichols, O.P., *The Realm: An Unfashionable Essay on the Conversion of England* (Family Publications, Oxford), 2008, 141.

64   Archbishop Augustine DiNoia, O.P., *Clearing Away the Barriers: Preaching to Young Adults Today*, Carl J. Peter lecture, December 7, 2009.

65   Pope Paul VI, Apostolic Exhortation, *Evangelii Nuntiandi*, 80.

66   Congregation for the Clergy, *General Directory for Catechesis*, 112.

67   Pope Benedict XVI, Address to the Plenary Assembly of the Pontifical Council for Promoting the New Evangelization, June 2, 2011.

68   Refer to Pew Religion surveys and CARA surveys.

69   Blessed Pope John Paul II, *Crossing the Threshold of Hope*, 1994.

70   Pope Benedict XVI, Homily at Vespers with the Bishops of the United States of America, April 16, 2008.

71   *Lineamenta* for the Synod of Bishops, XIII Ordinary General Assembly on The New Evangelization for the Transmission of the Christian Faith, 6.

72   Pope Benedict XVI, Address to the International Congress commemorating the 40th anniversary of *Dei Verbum*, September 16, 2005.

73   Pope Benedict XVI, Encyclical Letter, *Caritatis in Veritate*, June 29, 2009, 51.

74   Pope Benedict XVI, Address to Pontifical Council for Culture, 2008.

75   Edward Norman, *Secularization: Sacred Values in a Godless World*, Continuum, 2002, 44.

76   *Lineamenta* for the Synod of Bishops, XIII Ordinary General Assembly on The New Evangelization for the Transmission of the Christian Faith, 6.

77 Pope Benedict XVI, Homily on the *Solemnity of the Holy Apostles Peter and Paul*, June 28, 2010.

78 Edward Norman, *Secularization: Sacred Values in a Godless World*, Continuum, 2002, 170-171.

79 Documents of the Second Vatican Council, "Decree on the Apostolate of the Laity," (*Apostolicam Actuositatem*), 2.

80 *Lineamenta* for the Synod of Bishops, XIII Ordinary General Assembly on The New Evangelization for the Transmission of the Christian Faith, 6.

81 Archbishop Augustine DiNoia, O.P., *Clearing Away the Barriers: Preaching to Young Adults Today*, Carl J. Peter lecture, December 7, 2009.

82 Cardinal Joseph Ratzinger, "Mass for the Election of the Roman Pontiff: Monday, April 18: Homily by the Cardinal Who Became Pope."

83 Cardinal Joseph Ratzinger, Address on September 26, 2003.

84 Chris Stefanik, *Absolute Relativism: The New Dictatorship and What to do About it*, Catholic Answers, 2011, 4–5.

85 Cardinal Joseph Ratzinger, *Culture and Truth: Reflections on the Encyclical*, Origins, February 25, 1999, Volume 28: No. 36, 627.

86 Ibid., 3–4.

87 Congregation for the Doctrine of the Faith, Doctrinal Note on Some Aspects of Evangelization, December 2007, 4.

88 Ibid, 18.

89 Ibid, 38.

90 *Lineamenta* for the Synod of Bishops, XIII Ordinary General Assembly on The New Evangelization for the Transmission of the Christian Faith, 24-25.

91 Blessed Pope John Paul II, Apostolic Constitution, *Fidei Depositum*, 1992, 3.

92 Blessed Pope John Paul II, "On Catechesis in Our Time," (*Catechesi Tradendae*), 51.

93 Pope Benedict XVI, Apostolic Letter, *Porta Fidei*, 10.

94 Ibid., 4.

95 Blessed Pope John Paul II, "On Catechesis in Our Time" (*Catechesi Tradendae*), 52.

96 Ibid., 10.

97 Congregation for the Doctrine of Faith, Note with Pastoral Recommendations for the Year of Faith, January 6, 2012.

98 Blessed Pope John Paul II, Apostolic Constitution, *Fidei Depositum*, 1992, 2.

99 Pope Benedict XVI, *Porta Fidei*, 11.

100 *Porta Fidei*, 11.

101 Blessed Pope John Paul II, Apostolic Constitution, *Fidei Depositum*, 3.

102 Blessed Pope John Paul II, "On Catechesis in Our Time," (*Catechesi Tradendae*), 26.

103 The link to the online list of texts by the U.S. Catholic Bishops that have been found to be in conformity with the *Catechism of the Catholic Church* is: http://www.usccb.org/about/evangel ization-and-catechesis/subcommittee-on-catechism/upload/Current-Conformity-List.pdf.

104   Pope Paul VI, *Evangelii Nuntiandi*, 75.

105   Blessed Pope John Paul II, "On Catechesis in Our Time," (*Catechesi Tradendae*), 5.

106   Pope Benedict XVI, *Porta Fidei*, 11.

107   Blessed Pope John Paul II, "On Catechesis in Our Time," (*Catechesi Tradendae*), 22.

108   Blessed Pope John Paul II, "On Catechesis in Our Time," (*Catechesi Tradendae*), 14.

109   Joseph Cardinal Ratzinger, *Handing On the Faith in an Age of Disbelief*, Ignatius Press, 39.

110   Blessed Pope John Paul II, "On Catechesis in Our Time," (*Catechesi Tradendae*), 30.

111   Chris Stefanik, *Absolute Relativism: The New Dictatorship and What to do About it*, Catholic Answers, 2011, 56.

112   Edouard Cardinal Gagnon, presentation at the "Church Teaches Forum," Louisville, Kentucky, July 1, 1989.

113   Blessed Pope John Paul II, "On Catechesis in Our Time," (*Catechesi Tradendae*), 68.

114   Pope Benedict XVI, Homily at Vespers with the Bishops of the United States of America, April 16, 2008.

Bibliography of Resources on the New Evangelization

The New Evangelization and the Second Vatican Council

- Pope John XXIII, Speeches Convoking and Opening the Second Vatican Council
- *Lumen Gentium*: Documents of Vatican II
- *Ad Gentes*: *On the Missionary Activity of the Church*: Documents of Vatican II
- *Evangelii Nuntiande*: Apostolic Exhortation of Pope Paul VI

Blessed Pope John Paul II and the New Evangelization

- To the Assembly of CELAM in Port-au-Prince, Haiti, "The Task of the Latin American Bishops," *Origins* 12 (March 24, 1983), pp. 659–62
- *Catechesi Tradendae*: Apostolic Exhortation of Blessed Pope John Paul II, *On Catechesis in Our Time* (1979)
- *Christifideles laici*: Post-Synodal Apostolic Exhortation of Blessed Pope John Paul II (1988)
- *Redemptoris Missio*: Encyclical Letter of Blessed Pope John Paul II (1990)
- *Tertio Millennio Adveniente*: Apostolic Letter of Blessed Pope John Paul II (1994)
- *Ecclesia in America*: Post-Synodal Apostolic Exhortation of Blessed Pope John Paul II (1999)
- *Novo Millennio Ineunte*: Apostolic Letter of Blessed Pope John Paul II (2001)

Blessed Pope John Paul II and the New Evangelization in the Americas

- Address of Blessed Pope John Paul II to the Third General Conference of the Latin American Episcopate (1979)
- "The New Evangelization (Catechize at all levels)," Homily of Blessed Pope John Paul II in Mexico (1990)

- "Now is the Time to Take a Great Step Forward in the Work of Evangelization," Blessed Pope John Paul II, Audience with Bishops from Columbia on their *ad limina* visit (1996)

- Address of Blessed Pope John Paul II to the Bishops of the Ecclesiastical Provinces of Baltimore, Washington, Atlanta and Miami on their *ad limina* visit (1998)

Pope Benedict XVI and the New Evangelization

- Pope Benedict XVI, Apostolic Letter "Motu Proprio," *Porta Fidei* 7 (October 2011)

- "The New Evangelization," Address by Joseph Cardinal Ratzinger to Catechists (2000)

- Homily of His Holiness Benedict XVI, Papal Mass on the Solemnity of the Holy Apostles Peter and Paul (2010)

- "The New Evangelization and the Family," Pope Benedict XVI's address to participants of the Plenary Assembly of the Pontifical Council for the Family (January 2011)

- Homily of His Holiness Benedict XVI , Mass for the New Evangelization (October 2011)

- "Migration and the New Evangelization": Message of His Holiness Pope Benedict XVI for the World Day of Migrants and Refugees (2012)

- Message of Pope Benedict XVI to Bishops of the United States of America, Papal Visit to the United States (April 2008)

- Evangelization and conversion priorities of the Church, Pope Benedict XVI to Bishops from the State of New York on their *ad limina* visit (2011)

- Address of His Holiness Benedict XVI to the Bishops of the United States of America on their *ad limina* visit (2012)

- Doctrinal Note on Some Aspects of Evangelization, Congregation for the Doctrine of the Faith (2007)

- "Silence and Word: Path of Evangelization:" Message of His Holiness Pope Benedict XVI for the 46th World Communications Day (2012)

- Address of His Holiness Benedict XVI at the National Shrine of the Immaculate Conception in Washington, D.C. (2008)

- Address of His Holiness Benedict XVI to the Bishops from the United States of America on their *ad limina* visit (2011)

- Address of His Holiness Benedict XVI to the Bishops of the United States of America on their *ad limina* visit (2012)

Pontifical Council for Promoting the New Evangelization

- *Ubicumque et Semper*: Apostolic Letter of Pope Benedict XVI Establishing the Pontifical Council for Promoting the New Evangelization (September 2010)

- Address of His Holiness Benedict XVI to Participants in the Plenary Assembly of the Pontifical Council for Promoting the New Evangelization (May 2011)

- Address of His Holiness Benedict XVI at Meeting with Church Leaders Involved in the New Evangelization (October 2011)

- Papal Address to New Evangelizers, Address by Pope Benedict XVI (October 2011)

- The New Evangelization for the Transmission of the Christian Faith, *Lineamenta* for Synod of Bishops on the New Evangelization, 2012

- Address of His Holiness Benedict XVI to Participants at the Plenary Assembly of the Pontifical Council for the Family (December 2011)

Additional Church Documents on Evangelization

- *Go and Make Disciples*: A National Plan and Strategy for Catholic Evangelization in the United States (Spanish)

- *Disciples of the Lord: Sharing the Vision:* A Pastoral Letter on The New Evangelization (To the Clergy, Religious, and Laity of the Archdiocese of Washington)

- "The First Evangelization of the American Continent," Fr. Raniero Cantalamessa, 3rd Sunday in Advent Homily (2011)

Catechetical Resources for the New Evangelization

- *Catechism of the Catholic Church*

- *United States Catholic Catechism for Adults* (United States Conference of Catholic Bishops, 2006)

- *General Directory for Catechesis* (Congregation for the Clergy, 1997)

- *Study Guide to the United States Catholic Catechism for Adults* (Our Sunday Visitor, 2006)

ABOUT THE AUTHOR

Dr. Jem Sullivan is an educator and the author of two books from Our Sunday Visitor: *Study Guide to the United States Catholic Catechism for Adults* and *The Beauty of Faith: Using Christian Art to Spread the Good News*. For over two decades, Dr. Sullivan has served as a catechist in adult faith formation programs and as a teacher and professor of high school, undergraduate, and graduate students. She now serves new evangelization initiatives at the Blessed Pope John Paul II Shrine in Washington, DC.